RONALD REAGAN

A REMARKABLE LIFE

RONALD REAGAN

A REMARKABLE LIFE

J. H. CARDIGAN

ARIEL BOOKS

ANDREWS AND MCMEEL

KANSAS CITY

Library of Congress Cataloging – in – Publication Data

Cardigan, J. H. (Jim H.)
 Ronald Reagan : a remarkable life / by J. H. Cardigan.
 p. cm.
 ISBN 0-8362-0449-2 (pbk.)
 1. Reagan, Ronald. 2. Presidents — United States — Biography.
 3. United States — Politics and government — 1981 – 1989. I. Title.
 E877.C37 1995
 973.927 ' 092 — dc 20
 (B) 95 – 32715
 CIP

PUBLISHER WISHES TO EXPRESS GRATITUDE AND APPRECIATION TO THE FOLLOWING FOR PHOTOGRAPHIC MATERIALS AND RESEARCH: RONALD REAGAN LIBRARY; WENDY SPARKS; AMY EASTMAN; RONALD REAGAN HOME PRESERVATION FOUNDATION; STANLEY P. FRIEDMAN; JERRY OHLINGER'S MOVIE MATERIAL STORE INC.; PHOTOFEST; ROBERT EGAN.

CONTENTS

RONALD REAGAN

A REMARKABLE LIFE

PROLOGUE

On January 28, 1986, the space shuttle *Challenger* exploded just after takeoff, disintegrating in a ball of flame before a world television audience. This disaster stunned America: Never before had the dangers of space exploration been brought home so graphically. Because of intensive prelaunch media attention, the public had come to know the seven crew members with unusual intimacy. Now they were gone and the nation was staggered.

Then Ronald Reagan took to the airwaves. The president of the United States delivered a five-minute address that concluded with words written by a Royal Air Force pilot shortly before his death in the Battle of Britain: For I have slipped the surly bonds of earth/And touched the face of God.

President Reagan's short speech unified the nation. Tip O'Neill, Reagan's tough political adversary, with whom the president had had a fierce argument that very day, later described the moment as "Reagan at his best. . . . It was a trying day for all Americans, and Ronald Reagan spoke to our highest ideals."[1]

Memorial service for the *Challenger* space shuttle crew

President Reagan and
Nancy at 1984 Republican
National Convention

Reagan's immediate instinct was not to explain or excuse but to pay homage
to the dead and reaffirm America's determination to continue its space program.
This was what Americans needed in those harrowing hours after the calamity.

That these few words could be so effective says a good deal about a man
whose entire career—from his first job as lifeguard in Dixon, Illinois, through
his radio and movie days, and up to his culminating role as president of the
United States—has depended on his being in touch with the needs of people.

In going directly to the root of the shuttle disaster problem, Reagan exemplified what had kept him out in front for decades—a persistence of vision. His intuitive grasp of the situation displayed a capacity for speaking from the heart while at the same time capturing the emotional mood of millions; the people saw what Reagan saw because he was intimately aware of their experience. His speech drew attention away from the horrible specifics of the crash and brought out the nobility and sacrifice of the endeavor. Reagan persuaded minds aching with loss to concentrate on the deeper significance of what had happened—that seven intrepid souls had died in the service of a higher cause.

Seeing through the fog of politics to what the people are looking for is not a simple matter, but Reagan had an instinctive gift in this regard. It was the product of his earliest upbringing in America's depression-racked heartland, of parents with different yet complementary strengths and weaknesses, and of an abiding faith that, with persistence, any American could make even the boldest dreams come true.

In 1984 Ronald Reagan was swept into the presidency in the greatest electoral landslide America has ever known. Only one state—Minnesota, the home of his opponent, Walter Mondale—failed to go for Reagan. And that was by less than one percentage point. Reagan carried 59 percent of the popular vote and won a majority in every region of the country, every age group, and (with the exception of the unemployed) every occupational category. Sixty-two percent of men and 54 percent of women voted for him. Reagan also had majorities among every ethnic group except Hispanics, and even there his support jumped from 37 percent in the previous election to 44 percent. In addition, he was the first Republican presidential candidate to win a majority among blue-collar voters. Vincent Rakowitz, a retired brewery worker, summed up the general feeling when he stated: "He isn't like a Republican. He's more like an American, which is what we really need."[2]

What was this vision of Reagan's that so many people seemed to share? Certainly other presidents have struck similar chords with Americans. Franklin Delano Roosevelt, a personal hero of Reagan's, captured the passionate enthusiasm of the nation in 1932 and held it until his death three terms later. But Roosevelt served in a time of major crises—the Great Depression and World War II. Lyndon Johnson had the knack of discerning the people's mood as well as a common touch few presidents could boast. And yet Johnson was vilified and ultimately declined to run for a second term in 1968. Again, national affairs were convulsed by the Vietnam War and domestic strife.

Like both these chief executives, Reagan had a powerful agenda and succeeded in galvanizing the congressional and popular support needed to bring it

Giving a speech in Ballyporeen, Ireland, June 3, 1984

about. However, he also changed the mood of the country, and he did so with less help from such external circumstances as war and economic depression than any modern president. More than any chief executive this century, Reagan depended on his charisma to rally public support. Richard Nixon had a kind of anticharisma, an extension of his nakedly aggressive ambition, that won people over almost in spite of itself. Lyndon Johnson possessed charisma of the loud, expansive Texas variety that carried with it a tacit threat. But Reagan's own inner drives seemed almost invisible, as if he were not just an individual but a kind of average American writ large, a conflation of the roles of Hero and Everyman. In this sense, Reagan's achievement—and his appeal—is unparalleled. He dreamed big dreams and made them seem possible, just as his own progress from near poverty to Hollywood and then to the White House was a kind of fantasy made real.

Lou Cannon expressed this unique appeal succinctly in his 1991 biography of Reagan:

> But Reagan was a candidate of the future as well as of the past. He celebrated a nation in which an ever-expanding economy would make jobs available for everyone who wanted to work and enable all Americans to "share in a dynamic, exciting future." He believed in a world without trade barriers in which the United States would help create a gigantic common market. He envisioned a space shield that would protect Americans from nuclear war as reliably as an umbrella wards off rain. He . . . looked forward to the day when orbiting space stations would become outposts in the exploration of the universe.[3]

A new approach to economics played a significant role in Reagan's vision for America, and with dramatic results. As Reagan's policies were continued into the Bush administration, the national economy enjoyed its "longest . . . expansion in United States history."[4] Reagan promoted entrepreneurship, cut taxes, and pared government. Inflation dropped from an average of 12.5 percent in Jimmy Carter's final year to 4.4 percent by 1988. Eighteen million new jobs were created as unemployment fell from 7.1 percent to 5.5 percent.

This economic resurgence was more than a matter of statistics, however. Reagan had somehow initiated a sea change in the national mood, working an alchemy that turned the malaise of the Carter years into the famous optimism of the 1980s. Throughout his two terms as governor of California and eight years as president, this ability to see and respond to the people's desires served both Ronald Reagan and the nation brilliantly. Such an ability is not learned so much as forged by experience, and for this man that experience came early, in a part of the nation that had been the seedbed of presidents, poets, generals, football heroes, gunfighters, and inventors—the Midwest.

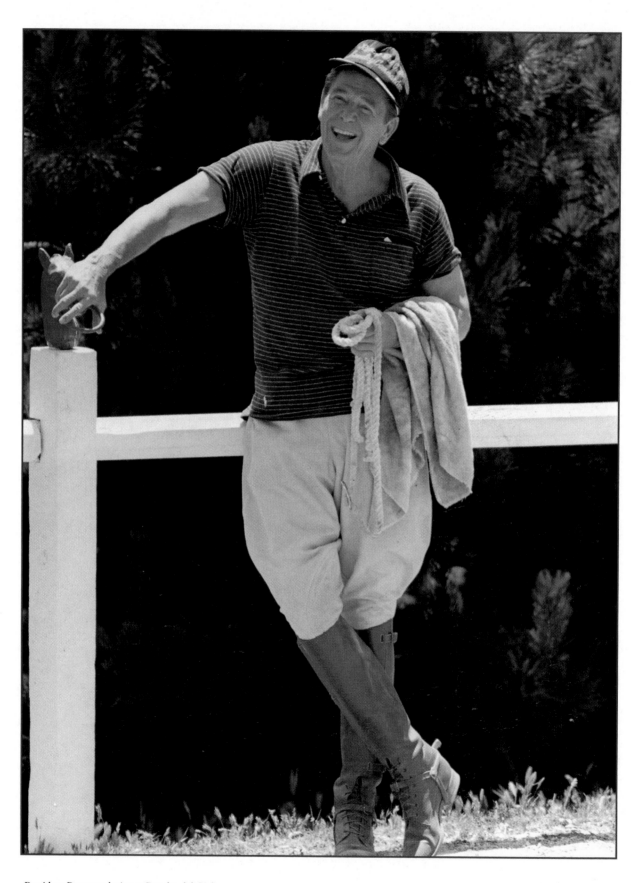

President Reagan relaxing at Rancho del Cielo

EARLY YEARS

I. Huck Finn Idyll

Ronald Wilson Reagan was born on Main Street, above a bank in Tampico, Illinois, on February 6, 1911. His father, Jack, remembered the tremendous noise his infant son made—and his size: "He looks like a fat little Dutchman. But who knows, he might grow up to be president some day."[5]

Reagan at one year with brother Neil in Tampico, Illinois

To read Ronald Reagan's account of his early days is to find yourself magically transported into Frank Capra's classic movie of small-town existence, *It's a Wonderful Life*. The vision can be instantly summoned by anyone familiar with the glory days of the silver screen. Of course, there's a reason for this—the simple lives and clear moral tales these films told reflected the way much of America thought about itself. Civic pride and virtues were taught without irony or argument. Church attendance was a regular part of small-town life. The information age was a long way off—people got their news from papers and even radio was in its infancy. The vast grid that connects the country today, from television to telephones, personal computers to the Internet, was not yet in place. The average home used an icebox, not a refrigerator, and the ice was delivered in horse-drawn wagons. This was small-town middle America in the 1920s and 1930s, with Ronald Reagan its archetypal product. He would later become both its symbol and its champion, a near mythic exemplar of America's Golden Age.

Tampico was not the first Illinois town the Reagans lived in and it wasn't the last. Jack Reagan was a clerk in the local department store at the time of his son's birth, but it was just one in a string of jobs that would keep the family hopping from one town to another for the next decade. Young Dutch—as he had been known since his father first applied the label—attended a different school every year between 1917 and 1921 as the family followed Jack's work from Tampico to Chicago to Galesburg to Monmouth, back to Tampico, and finally to Dixon, a smallish town on Illinois's Rock River. Even in Dixon the Reagans moved five times before settling down in yet another rented house.

Family portrait of Jack, Nelle, Neil, and Reagan at four years

The chief reason for all this moving about was Jack Reagan's profession. He was a salesman, a second-generation Irishman whose family had come from County Tipperary to flee the potato famine. He was not without higher aims, and indeed Jack Reagan had a kind of "burning ambition" to get ahead and improve his lot. Coupled with this drive was the personable "Irish charm" (which included a genius for telling stories) that would be his chief legacy to his son.

Jack Reagan felt the road to success lay in establishing a specialty, and to an extent he was right. In coming years it was in selling shoes that he had his closest brush with financial success. On the way to that dream, however, Jack would have to leap from one job to the next, honing his skills until an opportunity for independence presented itself. The Midwest had not benefited as much as the rest of the country from the sharp economic upturn following World War I, and in that climate a salesman's lot was unstable at best.

Despite his almost nomadic existence—or perhaps because of it—Ronald Reagan recalled his youth, in his own autobiography, as "one of those rare Huck Finn–Tom Sawyer idylls"[6] in which he and his older brother, Neil, played out a kind of fantasy Mark Twain boyhood. Reagan's clear-cut memories—even from those early years in Tampico—could come straight from "The Little Rascals":

> In a toddling expedition, my brother and I crawled under a train snorting steam in the station. We got to the other side just before it gave a mighty jerk and chuffed out. Our narrow escape would have been all right except that Nelle saw us. She nearly collapsed in the kitchen. She caught up with us as we were swiping bits of ice from the ice wagon (our target for the day) and earlifted us home.[7]

After Tampico, Chicago was the next stop for the Reagans. A gigantic department store called O. T. Johnson's was just opening there, and Jack had secured a position in its shoe department. Ronald Reagan's chief memory of the place is another life-threatening episode that must have tried his mother as sorely as the last. Nelle was very involved in the local church and frequently called away on errands to aid the poor. One night the boys came home from play to find the house empty: Jack was at work and Nelle was out making a charity

call. The boys searched the neighborhoods of Chicago for their parents and returned home to find their mother in hysterics. Before leaving the house, the young Reagans had been careful to blow out all the gas lamps, and now the house was filled with the deadly smell.

Galesburg followed Chicago, and it was in that nineteenth-century town of manicured parks and brick-lined streets that Ronald Reagan had his first intimations of the "scent of wind on peaks, pine needles in the rain, and visions of sunrise on the desert."[8] These visions took place in an attic, where young Dutch had discovered a forgotten collection of bird eggs and butterflies. The boy would sit for hours, staring at the glass-enclosed wonders. "The colors and textures—and most especially the fragility—of these objects fascinated my imagination. They became gateways to the mysterious, symbols of the out-of-doors they represented."[9] The intense imagination that would become so critical in his later ability to stir emotions in others was already forming in the young Reagan.

Reagan at eight years in his third-grade class picture, Tampico, Illinois (second row, far left, with hand on chin)

It was while in Galesburg, in his fifth year, that Ronald Reagan suddenly learned to read. He would later put it down to a kind of "osmosis," a product of looking over his mother's shoulder while she read aloud. "One evening all the funny black marks on paper clicked into place," is how he put it.[10] What was really at work is perhaps the key to understanding Reagan's special intelligence. He did not need to be tutored—rather, he seems to have opened his mind to the problem and, joining instinct with the powerful desire to make sense of the words, just "got it." Young Dutch was demonstrating an extraordinary power of intuition—a power he would use again and again on his remarkable path to Hollywood stardom and the White House.

However he did it, it was stunning. One day his father walked into the room and asked Dutch what he was up to. "Reading," his son said. "Well, read me something." When the younger Reagan did, Nelle proudly sped around the neighborhood to gather up witnesses.[11]

Reagan's Huck Finn idyll continued unabated. The family's next move was to Monmouth, Illinois, a town of eight thousand, steeped in the romance of its most famous son, Wyatt Earp. There Dutch came up against some hard characters, a band of kids who chased him all the way home from school because he

With the marching band
in Dixon, Illinois (far left
front holding baton)

was just "too new." Reagan later said it was the only time in his life he'd been "truly terrified, scared to death."[12]

Not long after this incident, and immediately upon the close of what was then known as the World War, illness rocked the Reagan household. Spanish flu was sweeping through Europe and America, and Illinois was suffering one of its harshest winters on record. Nelle was among the first to fall sick. She nearly died—millions of people did in 1918. No sooner had Nelle made her shaky recovery than Dutch came down with severe pneumonia. A doctor was called in and after a few days the fever broke, but it was Reagan's first serious ailment. No one was more delighted than he when, on the first day he was up and around, the very neighborhood children who had given him such a scare brought by all their lead soldiers for him to play with: "'The sun streamed through the window and I felt like a king with an army of 500.'"[13] Even today the president is moved by the sight of toy soldiers.

That this incident should mean so much to Reagan is telling. Although he could be bold in taking personal risks, Dutch was notably unaggressive toward his peers, a trait that may have been prompted by an undercurrent of disharmony in his own household. As the more responsible son, Dutch yearned for an end to family conflicts. This exhibition of friendship from the same children who had nearly beaten him up may have struck him as a personal victory—and delighted him as much as the sight of his own private army. A will toward compromise and a desire for concord would later become a hallmark of Reagan's

work as president of the Screen Actor's Guild and of his approach to internal White House politics.

Even though provoking fights was not Dutch's style, he was still a rambunctious youngster. In the next year the family returned to Tampico so Jack could resume work as the manager of Pitney's general store, and Dutch formed the West Side Alley Gang, but they weren't a very wild bunch. The point of their battles with the rival East Side Alley Gang was chasing them down and catching them, making them "lose face."

The Reagans were a tight family, and their closeness was reinforced by their peripatetic existence. This did not mean, however, that complete unison reigned in the household. Aside from the antics of Neil and Dutch, Nelle and Jack were divided on some important issues. Jack was two things that Nelle was not—a Catholic and a drinker. Although Jack had made a halfhearted promise to a priest to raise his children as Catholics, this commitment was overwhelmed by his wife's steadfast dedication to the Disciples of Christ, a Protestant offshoot that arose during a feverish period of religious revival in the mid-nineteenth-century Midwest.

Nelle was not just a churchgoer; she actively proselytized for the Disciples and mounted her own theatrical productions to drive home her religious beliefs. "She had a melodious voice, an ability to speak with conviction and she could quote the Bible at length. When words of comfort or hope were needed, she always knew the right and meaningful passage."[14] One of the most pointed of Nelle's convictions was her loathing for alcohol. This did not go down well with Jack, who was "wet" in a time and region where many towns were "dry" even before Prohibition. More than once Nelle lectured and scolded her husband on the issue of drinking. When her children became old enough for adult baptism, Nelle saw to it that they were brought into the Disciples of Christ. This experience had a significant impact on Dutch.

There were other salient differences between Nelle and Jack. Whereas Nelle showered her children with affection and attention—including nightly readings of such adventure novels as *The Three Musketeers*—Jack was often absent without leave as he prowled the town and whiled away hours at local taverns. What lessons he did teach his sons were sometimes of a more physical variety than Nelle's. Reagan recalls one episode in which his father found him battling in a

Reagan at twelve or thirteen years in Dixon, Illinois

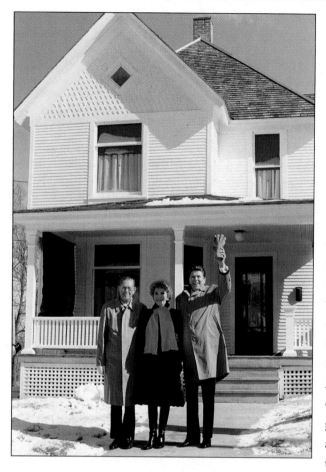

Nancy and President Reagan, with brother Neil, returning to the Reagan home in Dixon, Illinois, February 6, 1984

schoolyard amid a circle of onlookers. Jack stopped the fight, tongue-lashed the crowd, and booted his son into the air. "'Not because you were fighting,' he said, 'but because you weren't winning.'" Later Reagan would recognize this as his first brush with "adult injustice. I *had* been winning."[15]

John Edward Reagan taught his sons more than fighting, however—he taught them what to fight for. Jack was an ardent Democrat and a believer in the rights of the working man. When he cursed (another thorn in his wife's side), it was generally over such incidents as the 1922 Herrin coal strike massacre where twenty-six persons were killed when the police tried to suppress the strikers. As Dutch grew up he again and again saw his father railing against hotels that would not admit Jews or blacks, against the film *The Birth of a Nation* (which depicted the early years of the Ku Klux Klan), and against the Hoover government. These lessons were instilled early and deep, and they stuck. Jack's politics stuck, too—both Dutch and Neil became Democrats, an affiliation Reagan kept until 1962.

Nevertheless, young Dutch was drawn more to Nelle's world of church and amateur theater than to his father's man-about-town style. For all his roguish charm, Jack Reagan could be emotionally remote, a coolness from which Dutch retreated into his mother's warmth. He threw himself into the work of the Disciples of Christ with an unusual fervor, cleaning and repairing the church building, going to Bible class, and even acting in his mother's skits.

Nelle's passion for acting was reflected in her name, which she shortened from the original Nellie to become a kind of stage name. In the years before Dutch's birth, Nelle had aspired to become both a playwright and an actress. Over the years she communicated a passion for theater to her son, in whose early days acting was an ambition second only to football. Certainly Nelle's "melodious voice" and "ability to speak with conviction" were a valuable inheritance for Reagan—especially once they were blended with his father's storytelling skills. Believing what he said and saying what he believed were Reagan's greatest assets in both Hollywood and politics.

It was Neil who took after Jack—even to the point of parting his hair in the middle in the "Oscar Wilde" fashion his father affected. Eventually a kind of submerged rivalry developed between Dutch and Neil as their two very different personalities clashed sporadically throughout high school and college. To Neil, who was three years older, Dutch was becoming something of a sissy, a momma's boy; to Dutch, Neil seemed to be cultivating the careless irresponsibility that characterized their father's darker side.

A warm, loving, churchgoing mother; an engaging yet distant father with populist politics and a fierce ambition to succeed at his work; a close family brought even closer by financial hardship, small-town living, and a sibling rivalry— these were all part of an equation

Dixon High School drama performance in Dixon, Illinois

that added up to a kind of quintessential American childhood. But there were other elements to the equation. Despite the postwar economic surge that much of the country enjoyed in the 1920s, Jack Reagan's salary could not keep up with the rate of inflation and a local slump that seemed to be getting worse.

Nelle used what ploys she could to stretch their income. She would get discarded liver from the butcher for an imaginary pet cat, then serve it garnished with onions as the family dinner. Popcorn was another cheap staple—the family would sit for hours around huge bowls of it as Nelle read them novels and plays. Yet despite all this, the Reagans were strapped.

Partly as a result of this pre-Crash slump, Jack Reagan was forced to leave his job at Pitney's and assume the management of his own shoe store—the Fashion Boot Shop, which was part of the Pitney's empire in another town. In many ways this move represented an opportunity for Jack: he could be his own man and try his own methods, which included such technical marvels as the X-raying of the foot as a prelude to fitting shoes.

Dutch was nine when the Reagans moved to Dixon, the final town they lived in as a family, and it seemed a big city to the young Reagan. His experience of Chicago had been superseded by life in such tiny places as Tampico and Monmouth, villages of only a few hundred inhabitants. Bisected by the broad Rock River, Dixon was centrally located and boasted a population of over ten thousand. Though the family would eventually move to five different

residences, it was the house on Hennepin Avenue in Dixon that Ronald Reagan would forever regard as his "place to go back to."[16]

II. LIFEGUARD

By the time Ronald Reagan was enrolled in Dixon High School, he had discovered a passion for athletics. Since his youth he had played rough-and-tumble mutations of football, ranging from mass melees that resembled rugby to taut four-man games that chewed up his neighbor's lawn. Yet it was the varsity team that lured Dutch, and he fought fiercely to get on it. Neil had already made the team, but he had a great advantage in size. For all Dutch's impressive bulk at birth, he had grown into a short, skinny boy of 108 pounds who wore glasses. His only edge was in heart and determination, though he eventually made the team, being inserted as a guard during an emergency and holding onto the position when he proved his ability.

Just as he quickly grew to fill out his football uniform—he was over six feet tall and 175 pounds by his senior year—Reagan came to the fore in school theatrics. The drama club was one of his favorite extracurricular activities, and in later years he credited the club's supervisor with having a major influence on his development as an actor.

Swimming was another passion of Reagan's, and it was this skill that led him to his first serious job—lifeguard at Dixon's Lowell Park, three miles of wooded land on one of the more beautiful stretches of the Rock River.

Reagan saved seventy-seven lives in his six years as lifeguard, a feat that made him a local hero long before his achievements in radio, film, and politics. Historian Garry Wills, in his book *Reagan's America: Innocents at Home*, scrupulously documented this record—which wasn't hard to do, as Dixon's newspaper had made a habit of vigorously promoting the young man who had outgrown his spindly youth and who "had the movie-star look long before he was a movie star."[17]

Reagan always downplayed his lifesaving heroics, even grumbling about the ingratitude of the rescued—"I got to recognize that people hated to be saved: almost every one of them later sought me out and angrily denounced me for dragging them to shore."[18] But this is part of being a hero—Reagan was unimpressed by his own achievement because it was what he expected of himself. The young man was beginning to fit himself into the role he later played in Hollywood and carried out as president, the savior of the weak, the white knight. Taking on supreme responsibility, whether for thousands of swimmers or for millions of Americans, was something Dutch did as naturally as breathing. There was nothing to get self-conscious about.

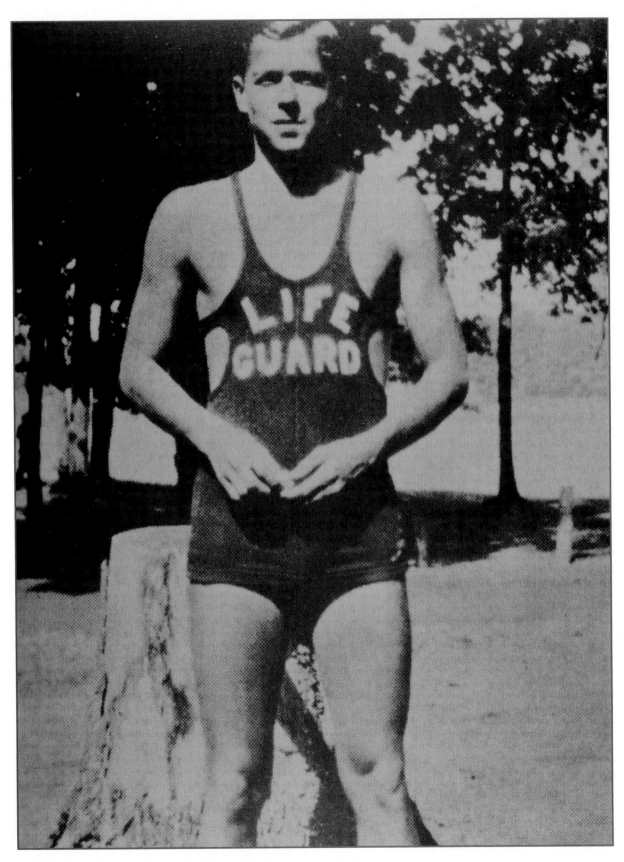

As a lifeguard in Lowell Park in Dixon, Illinois, summer of 1927

Dixon High School
football team
(first row, fourth from left)

The position was hardly glamorous. For six summers, from 1927 through 1932, Reagan put in twelve-hour days at his post. His labors began early as he hauled three-hundred-pound blocks of ice to the park concession stand—nine blocks in the high season. From then on Reagan bore sole responsibility for hundreds of swimmers, who often kept at it until after 10 P.M. But it was good money, two hundred dollars a summer, and allowed him to save for college. This was crucial, given the family's difficult financial position, because Reagan was determined to continue his education.

As rigorous as it was, lifeguarding gave the teenage Reagan much more than it took out of him. The long, active days lent his life a structure and stability that it desperately needed, because even as he nailed down good grades at school and even as his work with the Disciples continued—Reagan himself led a sunrise Easter service in 1926—his family life was coming apart.

One night, on returning home late from his duties at Lowell Park, Dutch came upon something that stopped him cold: his father lying drunk on the porch. The moment became a kind of Rubicon for Reagan as he struggled with the desire to pretend not to see his incapacitated father, step past him, to go to bed and let someone else deal with the problem.

That, however, was something the young Reagan simply could not do. Straining against his father's deadweight, Dutch dragged him into the house and put him to bed. In doing so he assumed at least a part of the mantle of responsibility in the household. Jack Reagan had been an orphan, raised under

circumstances considerably more turbulent and hectic than those he had provided his sons. Drink, for him, was a refuge from a difficult past and an uncertain future as well as from a string of failed jobs.

Although his drinking did not seem to have left much of a dent in local memory, Jack's behavior was certainly a defining force in the life of his younger son. Reagan recalls his mother's constant prayers for her husband and her seemingly contradictory insistence that alcohol abuse is a disease. Still Reagan remembers these years in an idyllic light:

Dixon High School yearbook picture

> There was the life that has shaped my body and mind for all the years to come after. Sitting in the Family Theatre, watching the marvelous flickering antics of Tom Mix and William S. Hart as they foiled robbers and villains and escorted the beautiful girls to safety, waving back from their horses as they cantered into the sunset. Weeping and laughing boisterously from the second balcony at the touring plays like *What Price Glory?* that projected real emotion from a shambles of scenery over a hushed audience. . . . Waiting and hoping for the winter freeze without snow so that we could go skating on the Rock River. . . . Swimming and picnics in the summer, the long thoughts of spring, the pain with the coloring of the falling leaves in the autumn.[19]

A major participant in Dutch's splendid life was a young woman named Margaret Cleaver. A "sparkling brunette," she was the daughter of the pastor at Reagan's church. When Reagan's best friend, Dick, Dixon's star quarterback, also declared his affection for Margaret, it was the church connection that gave the future president the inside track. Dick was only a Methodist. The potential triangle was averted as Dick conceded victory. Dutch and Margaret became a couple and remained so for the vital college years that followed.

Playing football at Eureka College

AMBITION

I. EUREKA

If lifeguarding proved a refuge for Reagan, college was the Great Escape. Ronald
Reagan had set his sights on Eureka
College long before he ever saw it:
He started saving to attend when he
was fourteen and one of his heroes,
a Dixon gridiron star, went there.
Eureka was a Christian Church col-
lege of about 250 students, and its
classic small-town campus was in a
village of the same name, some
twenty miles from Peoria. Although
the college was nearly as strapped as
the Reagans, it offered Dutch the
best deal it could: a waiver of half of
the $180 tuition and the chance to

Eureka College (far right)

wash dishes for his room and board. Reagan jumped on the deal. In those days a
bachelor's degree was a lofty target—only 8 percent of Reagan's Dixon High
class of 1928 went on to college. Even Neil had eschewed the expense of higher
education and gone straight to work.

Once again football and swimming featured prominently in Reagan's school
life. Although his freshman courses included French, rhetoric, English litera-
ture, history, and math, his main interests were drama, politics, and sports.
Studies were simply a means to an end for the young collegian, and despite a
fairly consistent B average in high school, Dutch just squeaked by at Eureka.

The age of raccoon coats and "Twenty-three Skiddoo" had reached its
zenith. "Flaming Youth," as this generation was known, were rebelling on cam-
puses across the nation. Bobbed hair and smoking for women, relaxed dress
codes, and clandestine "hooch" parties were becoming the norm for college stu-
dents. Of course, Eureka was a church-affiliated school where even dancing was
prohibited, but the students managed to have a good time anyway, and the
serene campus seemed to open a vivid world of opportunity, a larger stage than
Reagan had known thus far. He was determined to exploit all the possibilities.

Eureka College
dramatic fraternity
(second row, far right)

One of these possibilities was politics. Reagan effortlessly glided into class leadership. He had the good luck to be pledged into a fraternity before his arrival: Known as the dramatic fraternity, TKE house eased Reagan's entree into both acting and his career in campus politics, during the course of which he worked his way up to BMOC status as president of the student body.

From an early age Ronald Reagan had demonstrated an exceptional ability to capture audiences. Whether it was in a skit in a church basement or one of his high school drama productions, Reagan's remarkably engaging speaking voice with its caressing baritone and midwestern cadence, together with his candid, friendly demeanor, won him admirers on a large scale. Because he was able to project a sincere warmth and naturalness—he was an excellent raconteur, like his father—Reagan held audiences spellbound. In the early days his voice even took on a kind of gentle Irish burr as he recounted an anecdote, adding the exact touches needed to bring the story home to his listeners. This uniquely important political skill served him superbly later in life—in Hollywood, as governor of California, and as president—but its most dramatic early demonstration came when he was just a freshman, during a period of great turmoil at Eureka.

Eureka College was, like many small liberal arts institutions in that day, terribly underfunded. As a private school with a small endowment, Eureka was vulnerable to the same economic pressures that had plagued the Reagans and other midwestern families even before the stock market crash. Eureka was particularly under the gun, however, because of its policy of radically expanding the curriculum in an effort to provide as many academic concentrations as possible. New majors meant new staff; new staff meant a higher payroll. Before long the college was financially overextended, and in the mind of its new president there was only one solution: cut back the curriculum.

For incoming freshmen like Reagan this did not pose much of a problem, but for many upperclassmen it would be a disaster. It was hard enough to afford four years of college in those days, but to suddenly prune the faculty and course offerings would have meant no graduation for many seniors whose majors would be cut. Obviously the faculty members whose jobs hung in the balance

Major Reagan Shobe Fischer Burkhardt Stayton

were equally threatened. To young Reagan and many of his classmates, the quality of education at Eureka was at stake even if their own academic careers were not. It was time for decisive action if Eureka was to remain a college of "excellent academic standing."

The solution sought by both faculty and students was radical indeed: A campuswide strike was called, with the resignation of the president as its principal demand. A meeting was organized to take place in the school chapel just after a midnight gathering of the administration. Reagan, elected to represent the freshman class, was asked to present the actual strike plan to the assembled students and faculty.

"I discovered that night that an audience has a feel to it and, in the parlance of the theater, that audience and I were together," Reagan later wrote. "When I came to actually presenting the motion there was no need for parliamentary procedure: they came to their feet with a roar—even the faculty members present voted by acclamation. It was heady wine."[20]

The strike succeeded: Within a few weeks the president resigned. Eureka's student-faculty rebellion was an unheard-of occurrence in its day, an ancestor of the campus radicalism of the 1960s. But for Reagan that first experience with an

Eureka College
football players
(second from left)

Eureka College
dramatic fraternity
(top row, far left)

enraptured audience was a transforming event. He had come to the rescue at a crucial moment and had rallied the people to a just cause through the power of speech. Piece by piece the young man was building himself into the hero he always saw in his mind's eye—Tom Mix, saving the town and then walking off into the sunset, the girl on his arm. By small increments, Reagan was becoming the myth.

Reagan was similarly affected by another event that took place only a few days later. He and Margaret Cleaver were still very much an item, and her parents decided to treat them to a performance of a popular antiwar drama, *Journey's End*. This touring company's production was the first really professional stage acting Reagan had ever seen, and he was mesmerized.

He "was drawn to the stage that night as if it were a magnet, astonished by the magic of an ordinary man convincing an audience that he was someone else."[21] In fact, he was so focused on the main character, a disillusioned young officer named Stanhope (played by Laurence Olivier in the London opening six months before), that he began to believe he was onstage himself—actually witnessing the action from Stanhope's point of view.

This discovery, together with the arrival of an intense new acting teacher at Eureka, planted the seeds of real ambition in Reagan. Before this he had merely followed his convictions and done the responsible thing. He got good grades and went to college because it seemed right; he saved lives because they needed

saving. Now Reagan had a personal ambition—with all his soul he wanted to become an actor.

Margaret was a practical woman with more-pragmatic ambitions, and she could not take these dreams seriously. While Dutch put his studies on the back burner and concentrated his energies on the stage and football field, Margaret stormed the heights of academic achievement to become first in their class. Although even at graduation it was assumed by all that the two would marry, in reality they were traveling separate trajectories, whether they knew it or not.

As pleasant as it all was—the battles on the gridiron (Reagan was never a star for Eureka, but he eventually became a regular player), the picnics with Margaret and others outside the town, the swim meets and plays—Eureka was sweeter still because it was a respite. The stock market crashed in Reagan's sophomore year and the nation reeled.

Jobs, which had been scarce, became impossible to find. Reagan's own father saw the demise of his Fashion Boot Shop in Dixon and had to scramble for work miles away in Springfield, only to lose that job on Christmas Eve in 1931. Suddenly Dutch's summer lifeguarding job had to support not just his college education but his parents as well. To make ends meet, Jack and Nelle sublet all but their own bedroom in the family home.

Even Neil fled the difficult job market to join his younger brother at Eureka—a move that Dutch encouraged but led to a resumption of their sibling rivalry. Ralph McKinzie, the former sports hero who coached Eureka's Golden Tornado football team, saw an aggressive spirit in Neil that he did not find in Dutch. In 1985, well into his nineties, Mac recalled that "Moon [as Neil was known] was a natural player, fast, quick-eyed, tough to avoid. I knew he had varsity in him. . . . Dutch did better once Moon was on the team. . . . But I still didn't think he had it to move up."[22] Even in his last year in college Reagan spent most of his time on the bench, a second-stringer on a team that hard economic times had winnowed down to twenty-seven players.

But it was a dream that Reagan was after. Knute Rockne and Red Grange were his heroes, and Dutch was determined to join their ranks somehow. Typically, he achieved at least a version of this dream in the end, playing George Gipp in the movie treatment of the Knute Rockne story—a role he practically begged his way into during his early days in Hollywood.

Reagan had been seized with the notion of bringing the Rockne story to the screen from the moment he heard the tale of Gipp. George Gipp had been a star player for the Fighting Irish who was struck down in his youth by a fatal disease. As the story goes, Gipp made a deathbed request to his coach, football legend Knute Rockne, that some day, when the chips were down and the team was

Knute Rockne, 1940

faltering, he ask the team to win one in his memory. Playing Gipp provided Reagan with one of his most memorable movie roles; more significant, the very words "win one for the Gipper" shone a light on one of Reagan's own chief characteristics as president.

As Reagan had heard it recounted, Rockne had told his team the story of Gipp's deathbed request eight years after the star player had died. "If the story had come out of his imagination, no one—including Bonnie [Rockne's widow]—ever knew. To me the great significance was that Rock saved that story for eight years, and then didn't use it just to win a game, but used it to inspire a team that was losing mainly because of bickering and jealousy."[23] This statement reveals two things about Reagan: Once again we see his desire for internal unity and peacemaking to rally the troops against an outward threat. But what the story also displays is an understanding of the inspiring nature of a good story. Reagan felt deeply that the right words at the right time—whether truth or fiction—could have profound, almost magical effects when articulated by some-one who believed the underlying message with utter conviction. In the future he took a similar approach to the matter of anecdotes. Parables, for Reagan, moved mountains that no diatribe can budge.

Whatever Ronald Reagan began to see in his head and heart seemed some-how to take form and shape in his later life. He believed that any American could make his dreams real, felt it so deeply that the amazing journey from Dixon to the White House goes almost unremarked in his own speeches and writings. Whereas others might have used such a background as constant fodder for speeches or self-congratulation, Reagan saw in his unique career a great smor-gasbord of good stories and revelatory moments, not an object lesson or proof of divine favor.

Graduation at Eureka was marked by a special ritual—the seniors gathered in a circle holding a long strand of ivy that would be symbolically cut, leaving each student to face the next stage of life alone. Couples headed for marriage would have their strand left intact. Despite their rapidly veering courses—Margaret was headed to France for a year, where she would marry another man, and Dutch was intent on becoming an actor—the couple shared a strand of ivy.

II. RADIO DAYS

When Reagan graduated in 1932, the Great Depression was approaching its nadir. Franklin Delano Roosevelt had just been nominated as the Democratic presidential candidate, and both he and Herbert Hoover were crisscrossing the country in search of votes. Franklin was a ray of hope, illuminating a landscape

that seemed to get grimmer every day. He was met with wild enthusiasm wherever he went—whereas crowds greeted the president with cries of "Hang Hoover." Americans were ravenous for change as well as for programs that would inject money back into the economy. Roosevelt promised them both.

Presidential politics were not on Reagan's mind in 1932, however. He had been seized with the idea of becoming an actor while watching *Journey's End.* Now he realized that such an ambition would be treated as insanity in depression-gripped Dixon. Rather than risk this scorn, Reagan narrowed his sights to the field of radio. It was still show business, after all.

Over the whole course of his life Reagan had sought out father figures to fill the role of worldly adviser that his own father had abdicated. Sid Altschuler was one of these counselors—a successful Kansas City businessman whose two daughters Reagan had taught to swim while the Altschulers summered near Lowell Park. When Reagan asked him for help getting into radio, a fledgling industry, Altschuler had to admit he had no contacts in that area. Though he did give the young man a classic piece of advice: "Start knocking on doors, tell anyone who'll listen that you believe you have a future in the business, and you'll take any kind of job, even sweeping floors, just to get in."[24]

Reagan's response was to borrow the family car and head straight for Chicago, the home of the big radio networks. CBS rebuffed him outright, but NBC gave him a chance to talk to the receptionist. This friendly young woman informed him that his best chance lay away from Chicago, in the outlying small towns where local radio stations would be more inclined to take on someone with no experience. The drive home was a long and depressing one, and in miserable weather. But Reagan knew what he had to do. After yet another odyssey, this time to half a dozen small towns, Dutch found himself at the offices of WOC in Davenport, Iowa—seventy-five miles from Dixon.

The program director who came to interview him put him immediately at ease. An aged Scotsman who could move only with the aid of two canes, Peter MacArthur was, to Reagan, "a saint, but a show business kind of saint with a vocabulary that could crackle and scorch."[25] His eyes, Reagan says, put him in a kind of spotlight, telling him he was the complete focus of the man's interest and attention. MacArthur's legs had given out on the vaudeville stage, where he had once had a popular act. Severe arthritis had brought him to WOC, whose call letters stood for the World of Chiropractic. The station's owner, an eccentric named Palmer, was an early proponent of the chiropractic method—the station was on the roof of his school—and although he couldn't cure MacArthur's arthritis he did give him work. The Scotsman was now the voice of WOC and well known through much of the Midwest.

MacArthur gave Reagan a warm—if profane—reception but told him there were no jobs available; they'd just interviewed ninety-four people and filled the only opening. Then Reagan, his frustration breaking the surface, blurted out: "'How in hell does a guy ever get to be a sports announcer if he can't get inside a station?'" With that he stomped to the elevator, but the manager caught him just in time. "'Not so fast, ye big bastard. . . . Now what was it ye said about sports?'" Reagan confided his secret desire, something he'd kept quiet until then. He wanted to broadcast football games. MacArthur asked him if he knew football. Reagan thought he might, having played it for eight years. "'Do ye think ye could tell me about a game and make me see it? I mean, really see it, so as I'd know what was goin' on?'"[26]

From the early days of dishing out ice cream in Lowell Park, Reagan had loved to grab a cone and pretend he was a sports announcer, rattling off plays from mental tapes he'd made of actual games. He had done the same act from the sidelines at college football games, grabbing a wadded towel for a microphone and rendering plays on the field into vivid radio prose. Now he was being asked to do exactly this, but for a professional who might hire him.

The director put him in a curtained booth, with a microphone, and told him to invent a game and announce as if it were the real thing. Reagan summoned up a game he remembered well, a squeaker that Eureka had won in the last twenty seconds the previous season. "'We are going into the fourth quarter now. A chill wind is blowing in through the end of the stadium and the long blue shadows are settling over the field. Western still leads, six to nothing. . . .'"[27] He went on to describe Eureka's winning touchdown. The whole spiel went on for twenty minutes, and when it was done Reagan had no idea where he stood.

MacArthur was delighted at his performance. As it happened, the station had found a sponsor for the University of Iowa's games, and they needed a new announcer. WOC would pay Reagan five dollars a game, plus bus fare, to help do the announcing at the next game. If it went well, they'd extend the deal.

Reagan quickly accepted the offer. The money was nothing much, even then, but at least he was employed, and in the field he had set out to break into. The Iowa game was a great success. "An excitement caught me until I felt as if I were vibrating," Reagan recalled years later. "It was to become a familiar feeling, it never deserted me on any game broadcast I ever did."[28] He wound up announcing the last quarter of the game unassisted. Afterward, he was asked to broadcast Iowa's last three games of the season for ten dollars each.

Unfortunately, the station didn't have an opening at the end of the football season. Reagan headed for home. The following February he received a telephone call. One of the station's staff announcers had left, and Peter MacArthur

As WHO radio announcer,
1934

asked Reagan to take his post at a salary of one hundred dollars a month. His bag
was packed in no time. Show business had called at last.

In the fall of 1932 Franklin Delano Roosevelt was elected in a landslide vic-
tory, but he came to the helm of a badly listing ship. The salvage work had not
yet begun. Now all eyes were on him to save the country, and one of his first acts
was the creation of the Works Progress Administration (WPA). Jack Reagan had
been a loyal democrat and had worked hard for the party. His reward was a role
helping distribute food and government scrip in one of the earliest programs of
the New Deal. The job came just in time.

Forever after, despite radically changed politics and even a party switch,
Ronald Reagan was an ardent admirer of Franklin Roosevelt. He later explained
that he voted for Roosevelt "because I was a child of the Depression, a Demo-
crat by upbringing and very emotionally involved. Remember his platform? It
was all for states' rights, and it also promised to reduce the size of the federal
government and cut the budget by 25 percent."[29] Although few of these planks
are recalled today, every one of them could have come out of Reagan's own pres-
idential platform nearly half a century later.

In the meantime, Dutch Reagan struggled with his own budget nightmare, despite his huge leap in weekly income. Neil had fallen on hard times, Jack had not yet landed his job with the WPA, and Nelle needed as much support as her youngest son could provide. Out of his one hundred dollars a month Reagan had precious little to play with. Then things got worse—after only two months in the new job, Dutch got the ax.

Regular announcing, Pete MacArthur told Reagan, was not his forte. In sportscasting Reagan naturally injected a vibrancy that disappeared when he had a script in hand. His voice fell flat, and he seemed to be reading the text, not bringing it to life. Someone new would be brought in to replace him as announcer. Reagan wasn't an instant success. Even he agreed: "Nobody had bothered to give me any instructions on how to be an announcer. . . . I stumbled over my words and had a delivery as wooden as a prairie oak."[30]

This incident turned out to be yet another turning point in the young man's career. His replacement arrived at WOC but, as it happened, did not realize he was to be offered the position without a contract. He wouldn't take the spot under those circumstances, and before long Reagan was back on the job—though just "filling in." No one had to tell Dutch twice what was needed, and suddenly his on-air voice was sparkling and vivid, his radio ads riveting.

So accomplished was Reagan that he was among a select few staffers chosen to make the leap to the sister station, WHO, in Des Moines, Iowa, when the powers that be decided to consolidate the two stations in the spring of 1933. Reagan was joined in the move to Des Moines by his mentor, Pete MacArthur.

ROOSEVELT AND THE PEOPLE

In 1933, the year Ronald Reagan began his career in radio, novelist and historian H. G. Wells wrote: "The radio had been dominated by the president, and a certain hopeful imaginative generosity prevailed" (Garry Wills, *Reagan's America: Innocents at Home* [New York: Doubleday & Company, Inc., 1987], 105). The unique public appeal of Franklin Delano Roosevelt's radio presence influenced Ronald Reagan enormously. Though an East Coast patrician through and through, Roosevelt knew how to soften the harsher cadence he used for platform speaking and modify his distinctly upper-class accent while giving his weekly radio addresses—the famous "fireside chats." Vocally, he learned to become one of the people, even as he retained the full dignity of his office. At the same time, he could add a sense of drama and occasion through his splendid use of the English language.

The two gifts came together in what is perhaps Roosevelt's most famous speech of all—the declaration of war following the bombing of Pearl Harbor on December 7, 1941. Few people who have heard Roosevelt's delivery can read the words "a date which will live in infamy" without also remembering Roosevelt's stirring enunciation. His voice carries both the shock and the outrage that many Americans felt, along with an undeniable call to arms.

Ronald Reagan, throughout his political career, would pattern his speeches on those of Roosevelt, paying homage to the man who, more than any other, had inspired his unique political journey. Getting the words right, then speaking them in such a way as to maximize their emotional appeal, became hallmarks of his approach to the presidency.

The new post, won just three months after his arrival in Davenport, brought Reagan double his old salary and the title of chief sports announcer.

By this time Roosevelt's inaugural had brought a new mood to the country. Machine-gun nests had been required for security as the new president gave his now-famous address to the nation—"The only thing we have to fear is fear itself." Finally the long, tense interregnum between Hoover's defeat and FDR's assumption of power was over. The floodgates opened immediately as the new chief worked through the night to put the nation in order.

Meanwhile, Ronald Reagan was fast becoming something of a celebrity in the big city of Des Moines, whose population by 1932 was 142,569—double that of Davenport. The scope of the limelight that shone on Reagan had been widening by slight increments ever since his lifeguarding days. Eureka had seen that scope broaden further, but Des Moines was the biggest leap so far in Reagan's popularity. Almost overnight, Dutch Reagan became the toast of the town, a familiar of visiting celebrities and local politicos, one of Iowa's most eligible bachelors. He assumed the position with an easy grace, as if his earlier life had been the perfect training for such a role. In a certain sense, it had been.

One of his first acquisitions was a brand-new Nash convertible, in two-tone metallic brown. Reagan bought his jackets to go with the car's color scheme, and he began to affect a pipe—which he saw as a kind of responsibility owed the station's chief sponsor, a tobacco company. Because of his great personal appeal, Reagan was soon given the job of interviewing the many major celebrities who showed up at WHO, ranging from such sports giants as Max Baer and Ed "Strangler" Louis to stars of stage and screen like James Cagney and Leslie Howard. These interviews also helped fan the flames of Reagan's own celebrity; by the end of his first year he was well known to radio audiences throughout the Midwest.

Reagan's personal life also began to broaden and deepen. A cluster of friends soon formed around him, and they met regularly at a local watering hole called Cy's Moonlight Inn. According to biographer Anne Edwards, "Cy now had a large blowup of Dutch seated at a microphone hung on the wall behind the bar. Dutch would notify his friends of just what time he would be at the Moonlight by a verbal code at the end of his broadcast. At the Moonlight, Dutch Reagan reigned supreme."[31] Edwards goes on to say that "an investigative reporter could search long and hard and not find one man, woman, or child who disliked Dutch Reagan in the 1930s."[32]

Despite the repeal of Prohibition in December 1933, the Moonlight still served the kind of near beer spiked with alcohol that had been popular for so many years. Dancing to the swank music of big bands was the major pastime,

and Reagan was at the heart of it all. However, it was Dutch who acted as designated driver when the occasion demanded. Although Reagan developed a taste for good wine that he later indulged as governor of California, he could take or leave alcohol. He never forgot the profound impact that liquor had had on his own father's life.

Nevertheless, Reagan lived his newfound bachelor's life to the fullest. His budding celebrity enhanced a certain effect he had on women—a powerful magnetism that eventually helped him land his first Hollywood contract. At around the time he heard about Margaret Cleaver's engagement to another man, Reagan began dating a succession of glamorous, vivacious young women. None of them filled the void left by Margaret—certainly none led to a serious relationship—but Reagan's appeal to the opposite sex was now clear even to him.

One of these young women inspired in Reagan a passion that lasted a lifetime: She introduced him to the joys of riding. Although the relationship went by the wayside, the long horseback rides he had enjoyed with his friend led him to apply for reserve officer status at a nearby cavalry post. The one impediment to his commission was his poor eyesight, but with the aid of some good advice—by squinting through a hole in a piece of paper held between the fingers, an image comes into focus as through an ordinary lens—Reagan passed his eye test and won his spurs. He also won the right to ride the post's horses as often as he liked. Dutch was a born horseman, and years later, when World War II broke out, Reagan's first service would be in the U.S. Cavalry.

Among Reagan's other natural attributes was a genius for ad-libbing—a skill he put to excellent use on at least two occasions in Des Moines. The first occurred while he was reporting on a sport that had never been his specialty—baseball.

Like all boys then, Reagan had played plenty of sandlot baseball, but he had never witnessed a major league game. Now WHO was having him cover the home games of the Chicago Cubs from his cramped broadcast booth, four hundred miles from where the game was being played.

In the early days of radio it was an accepted practice for local radio announcers to create the illusion that they were actually at a game, whereas they were receiving from the stadium telegraphed bulletins that were decoded at the station. Despite the necessary delay, the announcer reported the action as if it were live. The man who decrypted the Morse code transmissions passed them to the announcer, who turned the bare facts into a smooth patter—about a pitch behind the real events—and included as much local color as he could muster.

Reagan was announcing in just such a fashion as a critical game between the Cubs and the St. Louis Cardinals was reaching its climax. Augie Galan stood poised at the plate with a full count and the game still scoreless in the ninth

inning when the line suddenly went dead. With no new incoming information available, Reagan felt he must keep the game alive: No radio audience would take kindly to a break at a moment like this, however temporary. "I knew of only one thing that wouldn't get in the score column and betray me—a foul ball," Reagan later wrote. "So I had Augie foul this pitch down the left field foul line. I looked expectantly at Curly. He just shrugged helplessly, so I had Augie foul another one, and still another. . . . He fouled for six minutes and forty-five seconds until I lost count."[33]

Reagan eventually got the news that the batter had popped out on the first swing, but the main thing was that he had exercised a valuable instinct that would prove critical in his future career—a natural grasp of how his audience felt at the moment, and the storytelling ability to bring an experience alive for his listeners.

Not all of Dutch Reagan's ad-libbing was in the name of entertainment. On one occasion not long after his baseball coup, Reagan's quick improvisation saved a young woman from a mugging. Des Moines was in the grip of a humid midwestern summer, and Dutch had left his windows open as he prepared for bed around 11 P.M. Suddenly he heard a scream.

A young nurse named Melba Lohman King had been walking to work when she was grabbed by a man who thrust what might have been a weapon into her back. The assailant made a lunge for her purse. Reagan was on the ground floor, not very far away. He acted quickly, shouting through the window: "Leave her alone or I'll shoot you right between the shoulders!" The man ran off. After throwing a robe over his pajamas and putting on slippers, Reagan escorted King to her destination. In a subsequent interview with a sports magazine, Reagan claimed he had a gun but it wasn't loaded. Melba Lohman King—who had gotten a clear view as he leaned out the window—never saw so much as a pistol, loaded or not. To her, it had been Reagan's firm vocal threat that had saved the day. "He was so strong-sounding in his command that the robber believed his gun was loaded—and so did I—and that was the main thing."[34]

In the baseball incident Dutch had turned a potential disaster into a field day by the same kind of free-form invention that had won him his sports job in the first place. Creating this kind of imaginative narrative would, in the years to come, become a powerful weapon in Reagan's arsenal on the speaking circuit and in office.

In a very real way, Reagan demonstrated this same skill when he came to the rescue of Melba Lohman King. He was able to create a necessary "reality" effectively enough to frighten away a mugger—at the very least loading an unloaded gun with words, possibly inventing one from scratch. The essential thing

was that he created the fiction to get a job done. And he seemed to infuse the dramatics with a kind of belief, a conviction strong enough to make the words ring true.

Perhaps the biggest break of Ronald Reagan's life, the one that propelled him, in the end, all the way to the White House, was his entree into acting. It came with the same apparent ease that seemed to attend his previous successes. The desire to act had had a place in Reagan's consciousness ever since his Eureka days, and this dream was, if anything, amplified by his success on radio. Reagan liked nothing more than thrilling—and connecting with—as large an audience as he could. Hollywood was a logical next step for a man in this position, but saying that and doing something about it were two entirely different things.

In any event, it was mixing with out-of-town talent and thinking on his feet that got Reagan his first screen test. The spark that flared Reagan's dormant acting ambitions seems to have been struck during a 1936 interview he

Publicity still, 1946

conducted on WHO with a woman named Joy Hodges. Hodges was a Des Moines girl who had hit it big as a singer, then been signed by RKO for a series of pictures. In the interview she hinted that Reagan might make it big himself in Hollywood. Around the same time, another singing act came through Des Moines and gave Dutch a similar suggestion. Al Clauser and his Oklahoma Outlaws were former WHO regulars who had been tagged by Gene Autry to appear in an upcoming western. Meeting Reagan in the course of promoting their movie, the group suggested that Dutch "come by the studio and see us."

A STAR IS BORN, OR
THE REMAKING OF DUTCH REAGAN

No Hollywood star of the 1930s walked off the street and onto the silver screen. Like death and taxes, the camera is a great leveler. Imperfections abound under the all-seeing, microscopic focus of the lens—and it was the studio's job to eliminate them. Reagan was no exception to this rule, as he candidly testifies in his second autobiography, *An American Life* (New York: Simon & Schuster, 1990):

I was playing in my first movie within a few days, but not before I'd played a spectator's role in an offscreen drama that might have been called *The Remaking of Dutch Reagan.* . . . First Stop: Makeup.

"The hair has to be changed," Max Arnow told a hairstylist.

The hairstylist looked at me the way a paleontologist might examine a newly discovered but as yet unidentified fossil plucked from a prehistoric riverbed.

"Where did you get that haircut?" she asked me.

"It looks like somebody cut it with bowl number seven," she added, before I could answer. . . .

They announced I had another problem: My head was too small.

"Where did you get that coat?" Arnow demanded, giving a fisheye once-over to a new sport coat I'd purchased solely to impress him. "You can't wear that outfit. The shoulders are too big. *They make your head look too small"*(81–82).

In subsequent conferences several decisions were made about Dutch Reagan. The first was that he was no longer Dutch but Ronald. Then it was determined that Reagan's neck was too short. The same was true of James Cagney, who was one of Warners' top stars. The studio solved the problem the same way it did with Cagney—through ingenious tailoring. All of Reagan's shirts were fitted with a special collar. The collarband was of normal height, but as it went forward it tapered down consistently, exposing more skin and lengthening the appearance of the neck. Reagan continued to order his shirts made in this fashion even during his presidency.

The matter of Reagan's too-broad shoulders was solved in a similar fashion. By having the actor wear wide, horizontally spread collars and the largest possible Windsor knot in his ties (which were normally narrow), the studio reduced the "gap" between his lapels, and his excessive shoulder width was effectively concealed.

Hodge's intimations and the Outlaws' offer were enough for Reagan. Now he needed only an excuse to get out to California. Somehow just taking the time off didn't appeal to his conservative side. He may also have considered it a bit unlucky (and arrogant) to go trolling for Hollywood success on his own cash. In any case, drumming up a deal didn't take long: "I . . . talked the station [WHO] into the idea that if they would put up the money, I would put up the time—and my vacation could be spent accompanying the Chicago Cubs on their training trip to Catalina Island. I made quite a pitch about what this would do for me in filling me with color and atmosphere for the coming baseball season. It worked."[35]

Ronald Reagan was off to Hollywood.

THE MOVIES

I. SCREEN TEST

Reagan's first stop in California was not Catalina. The acting bug was on him now full force, and after checking into the Hollywood Plaza Hotel Reagan headed directly to the Republic Studio, home of the Oklahoma Outlaws.

The studio was not overwhelmed by Reagan, and the feeling was mutual. Republic did not strike Dutch as the kind of operation that would propel him to stardom, and although they offered him a chance to read for a part, his instinct was to hold off.

The next day Reagan went to carry out his responsibilities on Catalina Island, but he was uncharacteristically lackadaisical about it. The island was a

Tugboat Annie Sails Again,
1940

famous resort by then, a Hollywood watering hole with plenty of distractions for a starstruck young man. Dutch took full advantage of the beautiful beaches and delightful scenery, taking it in stride when the Cubs manager, Charley Grimm, bawled him out for goofing off. "Some of Nelle's fey quality regarding hunches rubbed off on me. . . . How could I tell him that somewhere within myself was the knowledge I would no longer be a sports announcer?"[36]

After two weeks of what was essentially a vacation, Reagan returned to the mainland and sought out Joy Hodges to ask her advice. The singer was appearing that night at the Biltmore Bowl. Reagan showed up for her show and afterward sent a note to her dressing room asking for a moment of her time. Hodges obliged and came quickly to the point. She didn't feel qualified to tell Reagan whether or not Hollywood was for him, but she could help him out: "'I know an agent who will be honest with you. If we're wrong, and you should forget this idea, he'll tell you. Will you see him if I make a date with him?'"[37] Reagan would. At ten the next morning he was in the Los Angeles offices of Bill Meiklejohn.

Love Is on the Air with
Cliff Saum, June Travis,
and Eddie Acuff,
1937

Reagan later wrote: "He asked me questions about my experience, and I decided a little lying in a good cause wouldn't hurt, so the Eureka Dramatic Club became a professional stock company. I doubled my salary and finally, unable to stand it, I said, 'Look, Joy told me that you would level with me. Should I go back to Des Moines and forget this, or what do I do?'" Instead of answering, Meiklejohn picked up the phone and dialed Max Arnow at Warner Brothers Studios—"the only casting director in town who has the power to say yes or no," he told Reagan. When Arnow answered, the agent told him, "Max, I have another Robert Taylor sitting in my office." Taylor was currently one of the hottest male leads in Hollywood. Although Arnow told Meiklejohn that "'God made only one Robert Taylor,'" he was still anxious to have Reagan tested. An appointment was made. [38]

Once the pair got down to Warner Brothers, a couple of hours of poking and prodding were all it took to see that Reagan fulfilled the outward specifications of stardom. He was handsome in the solid, masculine manner required for a particular sort of romantic lead, which the studios felt appealed mainly to young girls and older women. His shoulders were broad—almost too broad—and he

The Cowboy from Brooklyn
with Dick Powell and
Pat O'Brien, 1938

was tall and well built. Just about everything else—strange haircut, wrong hair color, short neck, a lazy eye, the dent on the bridge of his nose from wearing glasses—could be fixed by intensive work on the part of the makeup and wardrobe people. What remained uncertain was whether he had any actual acting talent.

A screen test for Warner Brothers was scheduled for the following Tuesday. In the meantime, Meiklejohn arranged for a test at Paramount, but after arriving in the early morning and spending hours getting into makeup, Reagan was told the test might not be made until late that night. He would not stand for it. "'Son, this is Hollywood,'" the casting director said. "'Well, this is Des Moines,'" Reagan replied, "'and you can shove Hollywood.'"[39]

The Tuesday test for Warners went well. Reagan had been lucky in the choice of script, a light comedy called *Holiday* that suited his talents perfectly (Katharine Hepburn read from the same script in her own Warners screen test), and even though he later winced while watching it, his essential qualities came through, particularly his voice. Reagan later speculated about how different

Angels Wash Their Faces
with the Dead End Kids,
1939

things might have been if Arnow had not had such faith in his voice, because for the first few weeks of his career it seemed to be the only thing he had going for him.

When asked to stay in town until Jack Warner could view the test, Reagan again flew in the face of Hollywood. The Cubs' opening game was coming up and it was time to return to Iowa. Over Meiklejohn's protests Reagan boarded the train home and almost immediately began kicking himself. He needn't have bothered, for within two days of arriving in Des Moines Reagan received a telegram:

WARNERS OFFERS CONTRACT SEVEN YEARS STOP ONE YEAR OPTION STOP
STARTING $200 A WEEK STOP WHAT SHALL I DO MEIKLEJOHN

Reagan's reply was brief:

SIGN BEFORE THEY CHANGE THEIR MINDS DUTCH REAGAN[40]

It was a classic exchange, the archetypal summons to Hollywood, and Reagan responded in time-honored fashion by throwing his belongings into the

Nash convertible and heading west just as soon as he could. The good-byes at WHO had been heartfelt, but tinged with awe at the same time. Before their very eyes Dutch's old cronies saw their friend undergo a metamorphosis: "If those months of rejection after my graduation from Eureka were the low point of my life," Reagan later recalled, "that trip across the country, with the top of my car open to the wind and the sun shining on my head, was one of the highest of the highs."[41]

Reagan pulled into Los Angeles on the last day of May 1937. His eyes were red-rimmed after a drive of twenty-four hours straight across the desert, his linen suit limp with the heat. At his meeting with Warners the following morning he faced the next stage in his transformation—the inevitable Hollywood name change. After toying with a whole range of possibilities, the public-relations people finally came back to his full legal name, which he hadn't used in years.

Juke Girl with Ann Sheridan and George Tobias, 1942

No longer, the studio decided, would Reagan go by Dutch. Ronald Reagan sounded more euphonious, more suited to the romantic lead into which Warners had determined to mold him.

The studio system was in full force then. Once the actors signed the company contract, their lives were turned over to the studio in a fundamental way. How they dressed, where and with whom they were seen, which films they would play in and which roles they would take, what their hair color and even their personalities would be—as conveyed to the media—all, at least to some extent, were dictated by the studio. The degree to which actors played along with this system varied, but most—including Reagan—did whatever the studio asked. Once they had signed on the dotted line, they felt obliged.

Reagan's contract, which went into effect on June 1, turned out to have powerful resonances for his future career, but not through any of its specifics— it was classic studio boilerplate. Rather, it was the basic inequity of the contract that later propelled Reagan in a whole new direction.

Cattle Queen of Montana
with Barbara Stanwyck,
1954

In those days contract players could be fired after six months. If their option was renewed, they had another half year of security. The studio, however, maintained control of the actor's career for a period of years. If they wished, they could lay actors off at intervals, without pay, then later tack that downtime onto the end of the contract. In this way a seven-year contract could remain in effect for much longer, even after an individual had achieved star status. The studio could also rent actors out to other movie companies at their own discretion—often without the player's consent. The lending studio then collected the going rate for that actor from the borrower, while paying the actor at the contract rate. At one point in the early 1940s, Warners was renting out actress Ida Lupino to other studios for a fee of seventy-five thousand dollars per movie but paying her only her contractual fifteen thousand dollars a film.

Reagan was never comfortable with this situation, although in the beginning he was too concerned about making it at all to think about the future. Later, when his position was more secure, it was the unfairness of the studio contracts that drove Reagan to become president of the Screen Actors Guild.

Law and Order,
1953

*She's Working Her Way through
College* with Virginia Mayo,
1952

II. ERROLL FLYNN OF THE B'S

When Reagan made his debut at Warners, Hollywood studios produced two classes of films—the A's and the B's. The A's were the top-flight films, ninety-minute features with involved plots and thorough characterizations—and major starring roles. The B's, sometimes called programmers, were generally about an hour long and had shallower stories often driven by comedy, mystery, or adventure. A's tended to be

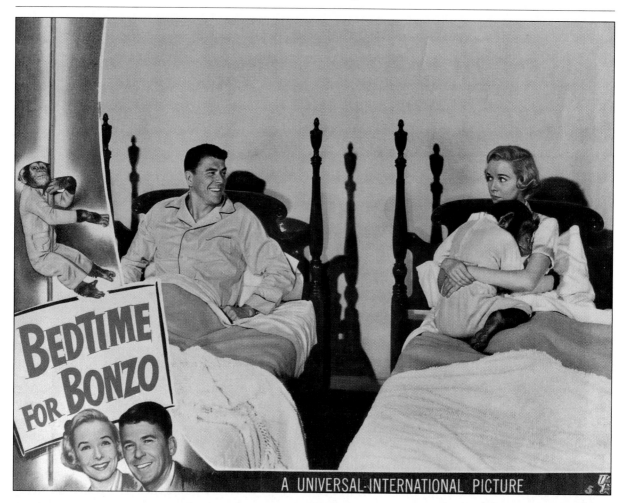

Movie poster for *Bedtime for Bonzo* featuring Reagan, Diana Lynn, and Bonzo, 1951

run on weekends, whereas B's filled out double bills and kept the theaters going during the weekdays. Based on his screen test and the studio's needs at the time, Reagan was slated to be groomed for the A's. But like any other new talent, he first had to prove himself in the B's.

Reagan's first film provided him with as gentle a segue from his former career as fate could have arranged—he played a radio announcer. Shot within his first month in Hollywood, *Love Is on the Air* was a light B comedy, and it was kindly received by the media. *The Hollywood Reporter,* a trade magazine, hailed Reagan as "a natural, giving one of the best first picture performances Hollywood has offered in many a day."[42] However, more important for Reagan, Warners renewed his six-month option and gave him a raise after the movie came out.

Ronald Reagan's first response to his new lease on life was to fulfill a personal dream by sending for Jack and Nelle, for whom he rented an apartment near Beverly Hills. Later Reagan's old TKE buddies, who had been part of the

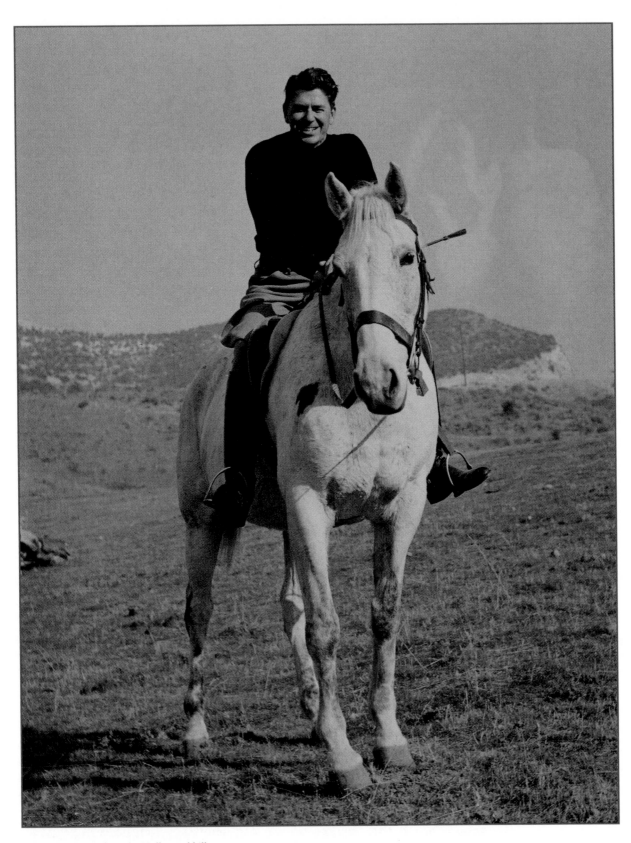

Reagan during a ride in the Hollywood hills

Code of the Secret Service with Rosella Towne, 1939

Moonlight Inn crowd, would also make the exodus, hoping to use Reagan's influence to get into movies. This influx of friends and family eventually exerted a considerable influence on his life and career. Although Reagan provided all of them with financial support he could barely afford, his midwestern allies in turn gave him the emotional continuity he had been lacking in the months before they came. With his cheering section reconstituted in Los Angeles, Reagan could meet his old friends for drinks at Barney's Beanery, a local haunt, and reestablish ties that helped him adjust to his new role as a Hollywood neophyte after being the center of attention in Des Moines.

Reagan himself lived in a tiny studio at the Montecito Apartments on Hollywood Boulevard. From his windows he could see all the movieland icons that meant so much to him: Grauman's Chinese Theatre, Schwab's Drugstore, Sunset Boulevard, and the Garden of Allah. Just a few months after moving in, Reagan, at the behest of the studios, escorted Lana Turner to the premiere of *Jezebel* at Grauman's, dressed respectively in tuxedo and ball gown courtesy of the Warners wardrobe department. Although Reagan hired a cab for the event, too embarrassed to drive his humble Nash, it was yet another slice of the Hollywood dream he cherished for the rest of his life.

Immediately after shooting his first feature, Reagan went to work on *Sergeant Murphy,* a story (about a cavalry horse) for which life had also prepared him. Reagan's love of horses grew to become a major theme in his life, as both hobby and therapy. For the rest of his Hollywood career he campaigned heavily for parts in boots-and-saddles–type westerns.

Reagan made thirteen movies in his first eighteen months in Hollywood. He freely admitted that many of his B films were poor stuff, but he took pride in a few of them. After all, he was getting to play the lead, even if it meant being, as he often put it, the "Erroll Flynn of the B's."

One of his most memorable characters, which he played through a number of films, was Lt. Brass Bancroft. A response to the then-current rage for government agents toting tommy guns—the G-men—Bancroft fought spies and smugglers in a series of action-packed programmers. In such films as *Murder in the Air, Smashing the Money Ring, Secret Service of the Air,* and *Code of the Secret Service* (so terrible that Warners promised the director, Bryan Foy, they would never release it, then reneged and released it anyway), Reagan battled the bad

Smashing the Money Ring,
1939

guys in prisons, in the water, in airplanes, and even once in a downed dirigible.

Critics applauded Reagan's performances in these pictures, citing his charm and vitality—and his ability to use his fists. But the young actor was also cutting his teeth, learning the intricate techniques of film acting. He was confronted with such challenges as "hitting his marks," in which the actor must learn to enter a scene and halt as naturally as possible when reaching preset chalkmarks; toning down facial movements to accommodate extreme close-ups; perfecting vocal cadences; and, more generally, working the camera. Reagan was a quick study before the lens, wooing the camera the way he won over crowds.

Reagan as a young movie star with his widowed mother, Nelle

In time Reagan earned both admiration and respect for his professional approach to acting. He arrived at the set sober and on time—key factors in the movie business—and did exactly as he was told. Unlike many actors of his generation, Reagan did not wrestle with his parts or ask for his motivation—a vogue even before Lee Strasberg popularized Method acting in the late 1940s. Reagan

Santa Fe Trail with William Marshall, Errol Flynn, and William Lundigan, 1940

Knute Rockne with Pat O'Brien, 1940

even did his own stunts. To directors these things were a godsend. At the same time, this smooth, workmanlike approach may have hampered Reagan's early movie career. He jumped on whatever roles were available, in part to support his parents and friends, and because he was so reliable he got them.

Although tough-guy roles almost made Reagan a matinee idol, in the long run they would have been a dead end. B films were simply not taken seriously. Such contemporaries as Wayne Morris had already broken into A films, taking plum roles that Reagan could probably have handled just as well. Yet because he was so intent on doing as many films as possible—no matter what their quality or budget—Reagan often missed opportunities that might have bumped him to the next level more quickly.

Breaking into A films required him to develop a different kind of character, for which Warners was grooming him and which was much closer to his own disposition—the gentle good guy. Reagan began playing these A- film characters even as he continued starring in the B's. In *Boy Meets Girl* he was thrilled to act with James Cagney, and even if his role (again as a radio announcer) was minor he attracted an enthusiastic response from critics. Later he was equally excited to join Pat O'Brien and Dick Powell in *Cowboy from Brooklyn*. Still, it was not until he made a cluster of successful A films that his new image was secure.

The first of these was a comedy set at the Virginia Military Institute, *Brother Rat*, which also featured Eddie Albert in his first big role. The film was a success, earning good money for Warners and stardom for one of its supporting cast members. Unfortunately for Reagan, the stardom was Albert's. Though his own performance had been good, movies rarely generate more than one discovery at a time, and on this occasion Reagan's luck wasn't in.

His next appearance was in *Knute Rockne— All American,* the story he had yearned for so long to see on the silver screen—with himself as the Gipper. The moment he read in *Variety*

Knute Rockne, 1940

Santa Fe Trail with
Olivia de Havilland
and Errol Flynn,
1940

International Squadron with
Olympe Bradna, 1941

that the film was going into production, Reagan practically battered down the door to play George Gipp (Pat O'Brien would be Rockne). At first the director was skeptical, for Reagan did not look to him like the classic football star. Even at 175 pounds he just didn't seem brawny enough. Determined to prove the director wrong, Reagan tore home and returned to the studio with a photo of himself in football gear. The point was taken—once he was in his pads he looked the role. O'Brien himself stood in for the screen test, and when the results were in, Reagan had won his first real spot in the limelight.

Reagan's performance, particularly Gipp's death scene, was just good enough to win him a role in another A picture, this time with Erroll Flynn himself.

Santa Fe Trail was just the kind of movie Reagan had been hoping for; he was back in the saddle in a western. The film was a historical kaleidoscope blending the story of the Santa Fe Trail with the rise and fall of abolitionist John Brown. Flynn played J. E. B. Stuart to Reagan's Lt. George Armstrong Custer. It was Reagan's first experience with rampant scene stealing, as Flynn, using every trick

in the book, elbowed his sidekick into cinematic obscurity. In one scene, however, Reagan fought back. It was 3 A.M. and as the cameras set up for a group shot around a camp fire, Reagan found that Flynn had moved deliberately in front of him. Scraping dirt together into a mound, Reagan built between his feet a platform that allowed him to deliver his only line from an eminence high above the veteran star.

Reagan went on to do other films with Flynn—including *International Squadron*, a remake of an old Cagney-O'Brien World War I epic updated to take place during the Battle of Britain, currently raging in the skies above the English Channel. It may have been this role that inspired Reagan, four decades later, to read the poetry that so affected the nation in the wake of the shuttle disaster—like the real author of those lines, Reagan's character perished in combat.

After *Knute Rockne*, Reagan's star had risen high enough that Warners arranged a loan-out to MGM—the "Tiffany of Hollywood," as Reagan called it. The movie was *The Badman*, but true to form, Reagan was about the only good guy in it. He later recalled the absurdity, foreign to the Warners lot, of wearing seventy-five dollar tailor-made Levi's that had to be beaten and sandpapered to look old.

Dark Victory, Reagan's first major motion picture, with Geraldine Fitzgerald and Bette Davis, 1939

When Reagan was cast in Warners' Bette Davis vehicle, *Dark Victory,* he found himself in a still higher class of film. Davis was at the apex of her stardom, and the cast included Humphrey Bogart, who was just beginning to peak. Despite this excellent company, Reagan never felt he had mined the potential in his role—Alec Hamm, a besotted socialite, friend, and confidant of the Davis character. This was chiefly because of major disagreements over character interpretation with the director, who wanted him to play the part with a repressed (or absent) sexuality. Reagan finally followed orders and played the character as the "kind of fellow who could sit in the girls' dressing room dishing the dirt while they went on dressing in front of me."[43]

What is interesting here is that when Reagan finally went to bat for a character interpretation, it was because the character he was asked to play differed from his own personality. This is vital for understanding his approach to acting, and it may be the reason he could go only so far in Hollywood. Reagan's vision of himself was as a hero, though heroes, by nature, are not conflicted. Great dramatic protagonists, on the other hand, from Oedipus to Blanche DuBois, are almost defined by the extent of their internal strife. Yet the very factors that limited Reagan's future in films secured his future in politics. He did not just *play* heroes on the screen; if that were the case, he could have played villains just as effectively. By his own admission, Reagan never portrayed a villain successfully. In his deepest conception of himself, Reagan simply *was* a hero. When a role abrogated that self-image, he balked.

Dark Victory, Reagan's first major motion picture, with Bette Davis, 1939

ANN SHERIDAN ROBERT CUMMINGS RONALD REAGAN BETTY FIELD

Presented by WARNER BROS. Pictures Inc.

Movie poster for *Kings Row,* 1942

That Reagan went ahead with his work in *Dark Victory* demonstrates his professionalism and dedication to his craft, but it also says much about the man. At his deepest level, Reagan was not essentially an actor; he was closer to a mythic character whose talents lay in making other people see what he saw, because he saw it with such conviction. At his core Ronald Reagan was not a born actor or a born politician. He was what he had always concentrated on making himself into, a kind of living legend.

Whatever drove Reagan when he acted, the studio decided he was ready to take on more important jobs. In 1939 he was offered what he later regarded his finest role, the part of Drake McHugh in *Kings Row.* The film had begun its life as a novel by Henry Bellamann, and its story was set in small-town middle America. Replete with incest, deliberate mutilation, statutory rape, and even imputations of homosexuality, the story was regarded as so sordid by movie industry censors that they warned Warners not to even attempt it.

To its credit, Warners plunged ahead with its adaptation of the script—though it was considerably toned down. Reagan's character, a small-town rake,

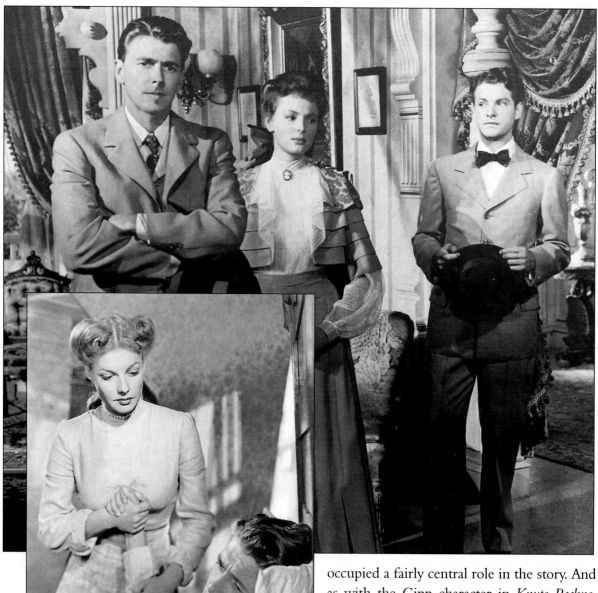

Kings Row with Ann
Sheridan and Robert
Cummings, 1942

Kings Row with Ann
Sheridan, 1942

occupied a fairly central role in the story. And
as with the Gipp character in *Knute Rockne*,
Drake McHugh had one fiercely dramatic
scene (once again in a bed) that captured the
public imagination and became a kind of icon
for Reagan himself. To end a romance between the Reagan character and his
daughter, the town's doctor performs a needless double amputation of
McHugh's legs when he is brought to his practice after a train accident. When
McHugh awakes from the anesthetic, he discovers what has happened to him,
crying out, ". . . where is the rest of me?" The line later served as the title of
Reagan's first autobiography.

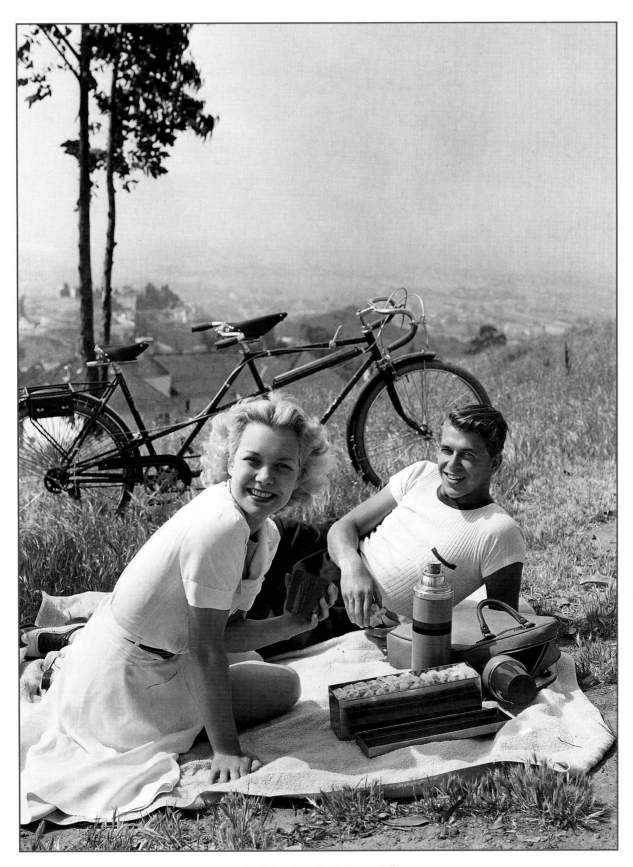

Reagan and Jane Wyman stop for lunch during a tandem bike ride in the Hollywood hills

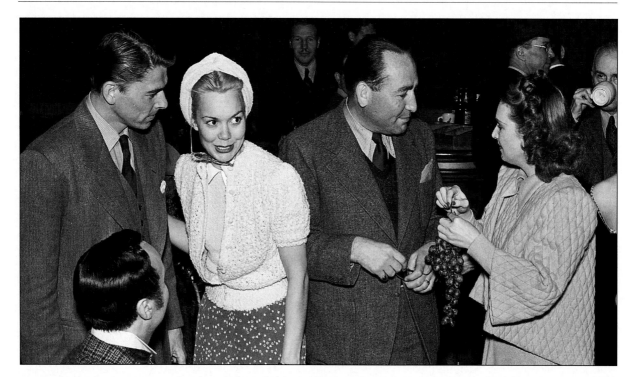

Charles Boyer (in back), Reagan, Wyman, Hal Wallis, Rosemary Lane, and Brenda Marshall at a ship's christening

In the midst of the Hollywood whirl and of demanding movie schedules that allotted just a few weeks for the making of a feature film, Reagan took yet another major step in his life—he got married.

Ronald Reagan had met Jane Wyman while working on *Brother Rat,* but at the time she had not been divorced from her estranged husband, Myron Futterman (the owner of a Los Angeles garment company). Reagan had been uncomfortable with the situation and kept his distance. Once the divorce was final, he felt differently and began wooing the actress in earnest. On their first date he took Wyman to a Sonja Henie film. Other dates followed, but it wasn't until 1940, after working together again on *Brother Rat and a Baby,* that Reagan and Wyman got engaged.

Although Wyman was celebrated as the classic "pert" blonde with loads of sex appeal, her background was hardly glamorous. She, too, hailed from America's hinterlands, but her family life had been troubled and lacked even the modicum of stability that Dutch Reagan had known. There was also a whiff of scandal to her past, which had seeped into the movie industry gossip machine. To Jane, Ronald was one of the few people in Hollywood whom she felt she could trust absolutely. That trust did not come easily. From the first she could hardly believe he was as good as he seemed to be. "'His manner was as kind, as friendly when he spoke to a waiter as it was when he spoke to a friend. The veriest strangers liked him on sight.'"[44]

The newly engaged couple were instantly seized upon by the studios as a match made in heaven. The hot blonde bombshell would be "redeemed" by taking the steady, traditional Reagan—six years her senior—for her husband. The first order of business was a whirlwind celebrity tour with the famed Hollywood gossip maven Louella Parsons. The tour featured the actors in a review of comic and musical sketches, with Parsons as mistress of ceremonies. It spanned the country from San Francisco to Philadelphia and featured four other actresses, one of whom was Susan Hayward. Although the review was not a critical success, the tour itself created momentum for the Reagans' Hollywood nuptials.

Jane Wyman

Jane Wyman

Reagan and Wyman's
wedding day,
January 26, 1940

Jane Wyman, in
You're in the Army Now

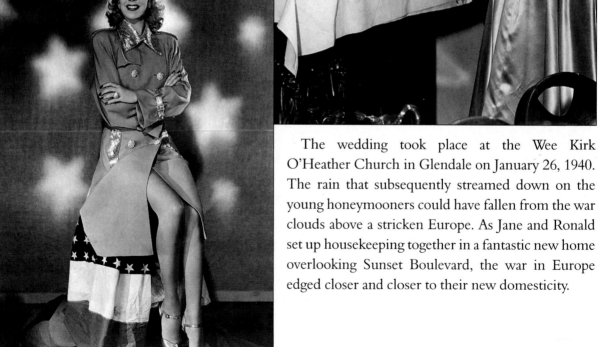

The wedding took place at the Wee Kirk O'Heather Church in Glendale on January 26, 1940. The rain that subsequently streamed down on the young honeymooners could have fallen from the war clouds above a stricken Europe. As Jane and Ronald set up housekeeping together in a fantastic new home overlooking Sunset Boulevard, the war in Europe edged closer and closer to their new domesticity.

Wyman and Reagan at their wedding at the Wee Kirk O'Heather Church in California, January 26, 1940

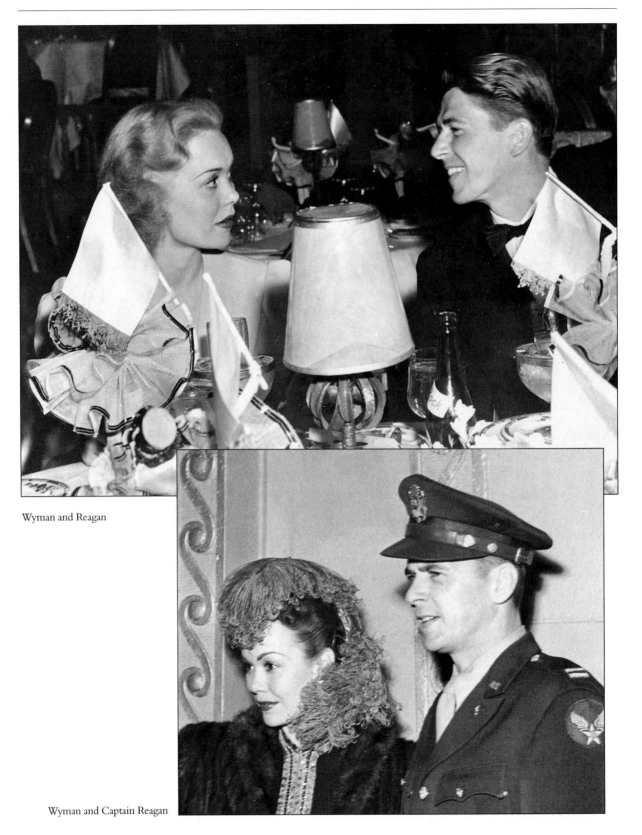

Wyman and Reagan

Wyman and Captain Reagan

III. THE SECOND WORLD WAR

As American participation in the war be-
gan to seem more and more inevitable, the
studios assumed that the actor's poor eye-
sight would keep him out of active duty.
But when Pearl Harbor was attacked on
December 7, 1941, all bets were off.
Within a few weeks Reagan was posted to
Fort Mason, near San Francisco, as a sec-
ond lieutenant in the cavalry. His orders
gave him just enough time to complete
Desperate Journey with Erroll Flynn—a
movie about RAF pilots downed behind
enemy lines.

Reagan liked the cavalry life. It was a
chance to wear boots and breeches yet
again and to enjoy the camaraderie of
other men as they worked toward a
common goal (even if that goal was chiefly
overseeing the loading of transport ships).
At first things were shaky with his com-
manding officer, who had taken a dim

Desperate Journey, 1942

Desperate Journey
with Alan Hale, 1942

Reagan with his mother

view of *Brother Rat.* Things were smoothed over, however, when Reagan wangled an appearance by Jeanette MacDonald for a base festivity. Soon it became apparent that Reagan's talent and Hollywood connections might better serve the war effort if he were back in Los Angeles. A transfer was arranged, and just a few months after reporting to Fort Mason, Reagan returned to Hollywood to begin the work that carried him through the rest of the war.

World War II was the most massive and technologically complex conflict ever known. To support the airborne aspect of the Allied effort, a special unit of Army Air Force Intelligence (AAFI) was organized in the world's movie capital. Effective training was essential to success as the air war became ever more vital to Allied victory. The AAFI unit was based at the former Hal Roach studios, which was unofficially christened Fort Roach. Most of the people who eventually worked there were movie types, many hired by Reagan himself, as one of his primary duties was rounding up the talent, even though the

Lieutenant Reagan with other officers and enlisted men at an Army–Air Force basketball game, 1943

bulk of those he brought in to the unit were several steps above him in rank. (Directors were generally given the rank of major, and Jack Warner himself was made a full colonel.)

Reagan with Wyman at an Army–Air Force basketball game, 1943

One of the key activities of this unit was to create briefing films that bomber pilots could view before taking on difficult targets, eventually including those on mainland Japan. By constructing highly realistic models, then filming them with voice-overs providing detailed information, the unit created simulations that enabled pilots and navigators halfway around the world to conduct dry runs of crucial raids. Targets were updated with each raid's damage to approximate as closely as possible to the real thing.

Reagan did the voice-overs for many of these films, taking the role of the commanding officer of a given raid and issuing precise instructions at each step of the attack. His soothing, authoritative voice was ideal for the part. As important as this aspect of the job may have been, however, propaganda was more vital still. Generating the images that would stir American passions and increase the homefront's resolve was perhaps the most important task before the warriors of Fort Roach.

To this end, Reagan made a number of feature films and shorts dealing with war subjects. The first was *Rear Gunner,* for which Warners assumed the costs of filming (film stock and development) while Army Air Force Public Relations paid for everything else. The movie was such a success at improving the image of rear gunners—it was widely regarded as an unlucky post—that the army promoted Reagan to first lieutenant.

In the meantime, Reagan still had something of a home life, but it was hectic. In 1942, Wyman gave birth to their first child, Maureen, and was managing the baby, the household, and her career as best she could. The studio publicity

Reagan and Wyman with their daughter, Maureen Elizabeth Reagan, at Warner Brothers Studios in Burbank, California, where Reagan was at work on *Kings Row*

machine cooperated with the government's propaganda services to help foster the impression that Reagan was one of those stars off in some far-flung hell hole, dealing death to the enemy. Whenever Reagan and Wyman appeared at some gala opening (they could usually get together on weekends), the studio would put out the word that Reagan had just "flown in" for this or that Hollywood extravaganza. It was all a part of the war effort.

The war and all its implications was a subject of intense fascination for Reagan. His political stance before America became involved had been in total alignment with that of the Roosevelt administration. He had argued fervently for the New Deal and just as fervently with whomever would listen for the president's prosecution of the war. In fact, Reagan's vociferous approach became a point of friction with Wyman as politics became ever more central to his conversation. Jane wanted to have a family and succeed at her career; Ronald Reagan wanted to change the world.

Reagan with his daughter Maureen

The Reagan family

Wyman and Reagan
dressing their daughter
Maureen, 1943

Reagan, Wyman, and
Maureen Reagan enjoying
a dip in the pool

Once the excitement of V-J Day on August 14, 1945, had subsided, Reagan began to contemplate the world this huge conflict had wrought. He had hitched so much to the outcome that it seemed impossible to imagine that a democratic utopia might not be at hand. The reality he saw changed his views forever.

IV. SAG

Ronald Reagan's political sea change was not accomplished overnight. The first step on his journey into conservatism was, ironically, taken when he became a member of the board of the Screen Actors Guild (SAG) in 1938. Wyman, who had already joined, encouraged her husband, but it was actress Helen Broderick who had convinced him to enlist in the first place, having "nailed [him] in a corner of the commissary one day at Warners, after [he'd] made a crack about having to join a union, and [given him] an hour's lecture on the facts of life."[45]

Even before the war, Reagan campaigned for the SAG with the same determination he had brought to the Eureka student strike. "It should be pointed out," Reagan wrote in his first autobiography, "that the SAG was as militant a labor organization as—perhaps more so than—most of the older unions. It had a comparably rugged early history. In 1933, when it was organized, 90 percent of the actors . . . got less than five thousand dollars gross per year. . . . All this before the deduction of taxes and 10 percent agents' fees."[46]

Despite his initial reserve about joining a union, the idea of the guild seemed like a fair one to Reagan, and his rapid progress to its top spot (he became its president in 1947) was in part an index of the depth of his devotion to just labor practices. At the same time, it was the SAG's central involvement

WORLD WAR II IN HOLLYWOOD

The tasks facing the warriors of Fort Roach were usually serious and demanding. But Fort Roach was also Hollywood; its troops were actors and directors, stuntmen and cinematographers. A few good-natured high jinks were only to be expected.

"For many years Warners had staged an annual party for all studio personnel," Reagan later recalled. "The big feature of the party was a film that was the talk of Hollywood. All during the year script clerks would quietly mark any take in which the performers had blown up or forgotten their lines—particularly if these lapses registered on film as profane or funny" (Ronald Reagan and Richard G. Hubler, *Where's the Rest of Me?* [New York: Dell Publishing Co., Inc., 1965], 142). At the end of each year this blooper reel would become the keystone of Warners' annual bash. In 1944 Air Force Gen. Hap Arnold requested just such a reel for the year's festivity—but no one had bothered to prepare one. It naturally became Reagan's duty to drum up a reel full of hilarious mistakes, and the simplest approach was to go ahead and make a movie, which he and his cohorts did.

"We wrote a script and filmed it just as we would any regular picture. I played a scene with a trick map that went rolling up . . . one of our high spots was a scene of a pilot—apparently flying a fighter plane at thirty thousand feet when a grip, carrying a ladder, suddenly appeared off his wingtip, walking in thin air" (Reagan, *Where's the Rest of Me?*, 143).

The reel was a fantastic success and Arnold had no idea that it had been concocted entirely for his benefit. According to Reagan, the film later cropped up on television and was acknowledged for the first time as the spoof it was intended to be.

This Is the Army
with Joan Leslie, George Murphy,
and Irving Berlin,
1943

This Is the Army
with Joan Leslie,
1943

in a major labor dispute that first prompted Reagan to open his eyes to what he saw as the greatest menace ever to face the United States—communism.

When the war ended, Reagan lost no time in rejoining the SAG board and doing all he could to distance the union from a set decorator's strike that had erupted earlier in 1945, breaking a no-strike agreement the nation's labor organizations had assented to for the duration of the war. That strike was settled, but Reagan had no idea he would shortly wind up at the SAG's helm during its toughest trial, an even bigger strike (involving the craft unions) that occurred in 1946.

In Reagan's own words, that dispute was "hideously complicated."[47] The account he wrote of it in his 1965 autobiography reflects this complexity. It is as if the essence of the squabble, rooted as it was in union jurisdictional disputes and money demands, was in some way sordid to him. Only when the wider ideological issue of a possible communist takeover arose was he able to exert his full powers—at which point he was effective indeed.

Reagan with Wyman after
the premiere of Wyman's
film *The Yearling*,
December 20, 1946

Night unto Night with Viveca Lindfors, 1949

Girl from Jones Beach with Virginia Mayo, 1949

Just as Reagan was not temperamentally suited to serious acting, neither was he the ideal head of a union. Reagan saw the world in broad strokes, looking for the heroic aspect of things. Unions are essentially concerned with economics and compromise, two things Reagan always edged carefully around. Like many who had grown up in difficult financial straits, Reagan saw issues of economics in an emotionally charged, moralistic light. Asking for money was in some way ignoble; people banding together in a bloc in order to influence economic issues had a petty ring to it. In order to square the reality of a union with his ideals, he had to see the SAG as the cavalry, galloping over the hill to save the downtrodden worker. This was, of course, not an attitude shared by many union members, who had created the union specifically to avoid the need of rescue at anyone else's hands. But for Reagan this framing of the issue was essential if he was to resolve his inner conflict and raise the fight above the level of self-serving economics.

Although Reagan was not in complete harmony with the gritty reality of unions, his inner conflict allowed him to distance himself from the heart of the bickering. Ultimately, this position helped SAG members and contributed to the strike's resolution. Because Reagan had stressed the SAG's neutrality in the strike, casting the actor's union as a kind of arbitrator between the producers and

the Hollywood unions, its actors were allowed to cross the lines and work without the resistance of other organizations. At the same time, this situation enabled Reagan to do what he did best—play the peacemaker between warring factions. "Reagan excelled at this kind of work," wrote Garry Wills, as "no one could bring quite the conviction to it that he could."[48]

The big strike began as a fight over which union controlled which workers. The International Association of Theatrical Stage Employees (IATSE) represented workers directly involved in movie set work, while, at the same time, dozens of other craft unions represented members who performed many of the same tasks as those in IATSE. Whereas a craft union might represent only plumbers or carpenters, the IATSE represented workers who often performed many crafts at once while working on movies. All these unions, and the SAG itself, existed under the larger umbrella of the American Federation of Labor (AFL). This brought a Byzantine aspect to negotiations, as the AFL recognized both the craft unions and the IATSE.

In 1946 the conflict, which had been simmering since the 1920s, came to a rolling boil. Word had gone around the industry that communists were trying to take over the IATSE as a stepping stone to grabbing still more power and gaining influence over Hollywood. Once the scheme was in place, the most effective tool for the influence of mass opinion in history would be in the hands of Soviet sympathizers—or so many at that time believed.

Communism had been a major presence in Hollywood since the turn of the century. In part this was a result of the influx of foreign talent that took place around that time, as early movie producers, directors, and actors transplanted European political ideas to sunny California. At the same time, because of the vast number of migrant agricultural workers in the southern half of the state, California was rife with labor turmoil—and with sympathy for any political notions that favored the rights of workers.

Reagan was in the middle of this in more ways than one. In his fervent liberalism he had joined a number of organizations that would later be accused by the House Un-American Activities Committee of harboring communists. One of these groups, the Hollywood Independent Citizen's Committee of the Arts, Sciences, and Professions (HICCASP), had movie star Olivia de Havilland on its executive committee. In July 1946, after a divisive meeting in which it became clear that certain members would not allow the organization's charter to adopt language explicitly barring communists from its ranks, the actress met privately with Reagan and a few other members. The atmosphere in Hollywood was so rife with suspicion that de Havilland and Reagan were equally shocked to discover that neither was a communist. Together, with a number of other prominent members—including FDR's

John Loves Mary with Patricia Neal and Edward Arnold, 1949

son James—the pair resigned from the organization. Reagan was making a move.

For months the FBI had been monitoring HICCASP's meetings. Now the government believed that Ronald Reagan might be inclined to work for it. In fact, after meeting with FBI agents and being reassured of their confidence in his loyalty, Reagan was more than happy to help the bureau. Eventually, both he and Jane provided the government with names of people within the SAG whom they believed to be communists. The FBI even gave Reagan a gun to wear, as defense against rabid party members who might make an attempt on his life.

In the end the strike was resolved, a denouement presided over by Reagan himself, as the SAG remained the central agency of negotiation. Once again Ronald Reagan brought together warring factions. He got on the phone with the representatives of the studio heads and agreed to a number of their stipulations in exchange for their acceptance of softened demands on the part of the Hollywood unions. In his mind, his concession was a matter of preserving the movie industry, and even the nation, from a threat that transcended labor issues.

John Loves Mary with
Patricia Neal, 1949

Reagan's stand during the labor negotiations had led to the juggling of intense emotions. On the one hand, he believed unequivocally in the rights of the workers involved to equitable pay and working conditions; on the other hand, he had become firmly convinced that there was a communist movement afoot to infiltrate Hollywood.

Just as significant, Reagan was unimpressed by what the end of World War II had brought about in America at large. All around him he saw evidence of a widening government bureaucracy, of institutions that he had considered temporary responses to the Great Depression and the war hardening into permanence. Income tax was another issue—perhaps one of the most profound. Reagan was vocal about his shock at finding himself in a tax bracket that had risen above 90 percent. More than ever before Ronald Reagan found himself talking politics to anyone who would listen. As the strike receded into history, he moved closer to making history of his own.

During the period when Reagan was becoming something of a real-life G-man, Wyman was cooling on their relationship. Now that her husband was seriously engaged in the battle to save Hollywood and possibly the entire nation, she felt more estranged from him than ever. In 1945 the Reagans adopted a baby son, Michael, but despite this happy addition to the family, Jane and Ronald were on divergent courses. While Reagan embroiled himself in the SAG and the battle against communists, Wyman poured herself into acting.

Jane Wyman in
Johnny Belinda,
1948

Jane Wyman in
Johnny Belinda with
Lew Ayres,
1948

In 1947 Wyman's career took an enormous leap forward with the filming of *Johnny Belinda,* in which she costarred with Lew Ayres. Ayres had starred years earlier in *All's Quiet on the Western Front,* the critically acclaimed film about a German soldier in the First World War who refuses to fight. The actor had more recently become famous as a conscientious objector and had wound up as a combat medic in World War II's Pacific theater. Unlike the soldier he played in the movie, Ayres survived the war and became widely respected in Hollywood for his courageous stand. Wyman found consolation in Ayres's company, and by the end of filming they had come to be regarded as an item in Hollywood gossip.

Jane Wyman won a 1948 Academy Award for her role in *Johnny Belinda.* Her escort for the evening was Lew Ayres, not Ronald Reagan, who attended on his own. Wyman accepted the Best Actress Oscar in a brief, graceful speech that took into account the fact that she had played a mute character: "'I accept this very gratefully for keeping my mouth shut. I think I'll do it again.'"[49]

Jane Wyman receiving the Academy Award for Best Actress, for *Johnny Belinda*, 1949

The Hasty Heart
with Patricia Neal,
1949

The divorce was finalized on July 16, 1948. Reagan joked to Louella Parsons about naming Johnny Belinda as co-respondent; but despite his bluff exterior, he was shaken. Later he cited his absorption in SAG affairs as a probable reason for the marriage's disintegration. Wyman blamed Reagan's politics, pointing to her annoyance at his proselytizing as the reason for ending their life together.

This was a rough period for Reagan. His last three films had been disastrous. Perhaps the worst of them, *That Hagen Girl* featured Reagan as the opposite number in Shirley Temple's first romantic role. The public was not ready to see its cute little girl grow up quite so fast—she was still a teenager at the time—and the script was revised to leave the conclusion of the movie unclear. Were they lovers or friends? It was not the stuff of great drama. In addition, the strike, though finally over, had been a victory neither tidy nor glorious. On top of it all, around the time of his divorce Reagan's leg was broken in three places at a charity softball game—an injury that, he later noted, cost him at least $150,000 in lost income from two films he was obliged to turn down. For Ronald Reagan, it was time for something wonderful to happen. And it did.

Movie poster for *Hellcats of the Navy*, 1957

POLITICS

I. NANCY

Nancy Davis
with her mother,
Edith

In many ways this second bachelorhood could have
been seen as yet another Reagan idyll. He had a per-
fectly situated apartment, a Cadillac convertible, and
the names and numbers of some of the most glam-
orous women in show business. However, the glittery
Hollywood social scene had never really been his mi-
lieu. Even when he was courting Jane Wyman, the rou-
tine had been more one of palling around with his old
college buddies, of sports and beach parties and horseback
riding, than of Hollywood nightclubs. Nevertheless, after a
brief hiatus Reagan was once again on the circuit. He dated the
occasional starlet, including Patricia Neal, and made a few more
movies—like *John Loves Mary,* which was Neal's debut—but it was not until he
rang the doorbell of Nancy Davis that love came back into his life.

Nancy Davis had a considerable pedigree in the acting business. Her
mother, the former Edie Luckett, had had a long career in stage and film, and
Nancy herself had been treading the boards since her childhood. She had come
to Hollywood from her hometown of Chicago in search of a movie career in the
late 1940s, and through the intervention of Spencer Tracy, an old friend of her
mother's, she had managed to get a screen test in 1949. It was not a stunning suc-
cess, but it was enough. For the next few years she played a succession of preg-
nant housewives, usually in comedies. As far as Davis was concerned, it was
better than winding up a postdeb in Chicago. Hollywood stardom was not
her objective.

According to Reagan, Davis had telephoned SAG headquarters with the
request that something be done to clear her name from imputations of commu-
nism. Apparently there was another actress named Nancy Davis who *was* a com-
munist, and she was suffering from the confusion. Reagan agreed to meet with
her, but only for a brief dinner because he had another pressing engagement. He
arrived at her home to pick her up and was immediately struck silly. The dinner
stretched on into the early hours of the morning as the couple talked endlessly.
The something wonderful had happened. At last, Reagan had found a kindred

Nancy Davis pictured
in the New York
Sunday News,
December 3, 1950

spirit, a woman who shared his political philosophy and was more than willing
to hear him articulate it.

The alliance Reagan forged with Nancy Davis was more than a romance or
a marriage—it was one of the most significant steps of his political career. With
Nancy by his side, Reagan finally had the companion he needed to complete his
vision for the future. Now he could move on.

Nancy and Ronald were married on March 4, 1952. Their first move was to
buy a ranch. For years Reagan had dreamed of owning horses and enough

acreage to ride. Now he could actually raise them, and on plenty of land; the area they chose was still open country at that time. A few years before, Reagan's agent had landed him a contract that would pay him a million dollars over the course of seven years. Ronald Reagan could afford to live as he wished.

In the autumn after their marriage, the Reagan clan expanded when Nancy gave birth to Patricia Ann. It was a difficult delivery, and Ronald, having resigned his post as SAG president, spent his time at home helping his new wife recuperate. Ultimately Nancy rallied, and in 1958 she provided her husband with the final

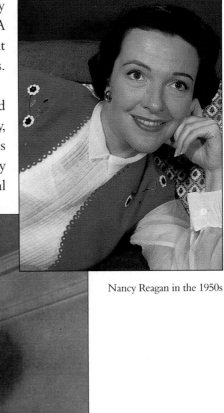

Nancy Reagan in the 1950s

Wedding Day for Nancy and Ronald, March 4, 1952

Wedding Day for Nancy and Ronald, with Mr. and Mrs. William Holden as best man and matron of honor

Reagan and Nancy with Nelle Reagan and Loyal and Lucky Davis

member of the Reagan family, a son named for his father, Ronald Reagan. Eschewing the usual "Junior," Ronald and Nancy gave him the middle name Prescott to distinguish him from his father.

Although Reagan continued to make movies right up until the eve of his run for governor of California, a new technology was on the rise and he had begun to sense its potential. Television would turn out, if anything, to be an even better medium for Reagan's talents than film. More intimate and immediate than movies, television was a direct connection into people's homes. Reagan's conversational style and gentle charm would play more readily through the small screen than it ever did on the big one. Once he learned the ropes, his appeal would translate brilliantly to the new medium.

By 1952 Reagan was represented by the Music Corporation of America (MCA), which had taken over Bill Meicklejohn's agency. His current representative, Lew Wasserman, eventually became arguably the most powerful deal-maker in Hollywood. It was Wasserman who had obtained Reagan's million-dollar contract, and though not remarkable by today's standards, it was an impressive deal at that time for a star of Reagan's rank. It was also the first time the agent had ever obtained seven figures. Wasserman agreed with Reagan that, although the agency had been doing its best, he was not being cast in the kind of films that would improve his career. At the same time, Reagan was concerned about money. The ranch would be a stretch even on his excellent salary, and he did not feel inclined to accept the offers Warners was currently pressing on him. Wasserman came up with a new idea.

As odd as it sounded, Reagan's agent wanted him to do a Las Vegas review. He would be the master of ceremonies, adding a liberal dose of his own anecdotal brilliance to an evening of comedy acts. Several weeks of this work could raise a

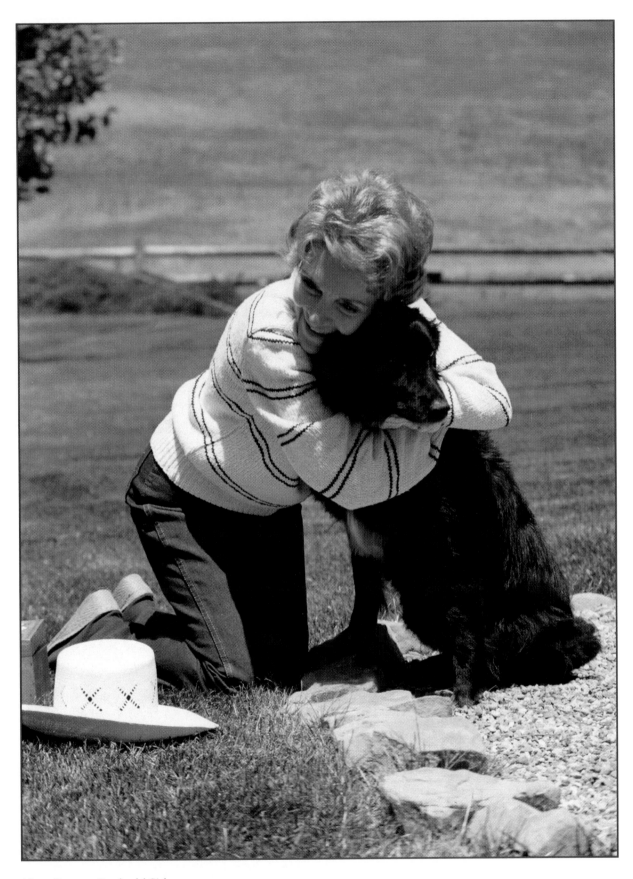

Nancy Reagan at Rancho del Cielo

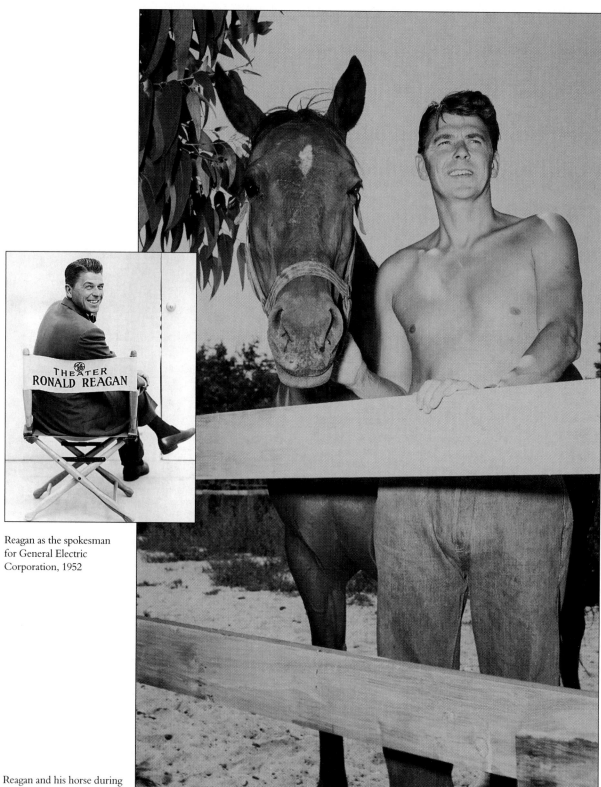

Reagan as the spokesman
for General Electric
Corporation, 1952

Reagan and his horse during
the Hollywood years

reasonable amount of money, and, although Reagan had never done anything quite like it, he accepted.

The show itself was a marginal success, but what it led to was pure gold for Reagan—the role of spokesman for the General Electric Corporation (GE), known more for its light bulbs than for its huge high-tech turbine engines and other major product lines. GE was a massive, emerging conglomerate in 1952, a company so diversified there seemed to be no way to give it a consistent public face. When GE executives learned that MCA was interested in helping Reagan find new applications for his talent, they seized on him as their new spokesman. After all, MCA was producing "General Electric Theatre," a weekly showcase for television dramas.

Like his marriage with Nancy, Reagan's relationship with GE would be a transformative partnership. For the next six years Ronald Reagan forged the text that would bring him to the forefront of Republican politics.

Reagan and Nancy at home, polishing boots

II. THE SPEECH

From his first years traveling around the country and inspiring GE workers until his bid for governor, Ronald Reagan delivered what he came to call The Speech to groups of all sizes and shapes and in every corner of the United States. In time the script became so focused and polished that he could fine-tune it for any audience and pull it out in any situation. The central theme of the speech was simple: America is gravely threatened by the expansion of government into every arena of private life, as well as by communist infiltration.

Pounding away at a few points rather than tackling hundreds of problems in detail, Reagan was able to create an image that was at once sincere and comprehensible to a vast audience. By delivering The Speech literally hundreds of times to groups of every description, from rotary clubs and factory workers to hundred-dollar-a-plate Republicans, Reagan was able to hone its edge while still keeping it fresh with updated facts and anecdotes. In *Where's the Rest of Me?,* the

Nancy and Reagan

autobiography he completed just before his official entrance into politics, The Speech forms the final chapter.

In essence, The Speech was a kind of warning to all Americans. Government was trying to take over our lives. The federal power structure, through its bureaucracy, its regulations, an inequitable system of taxation, and the sheer force of its institutions, was seeking to impose an unbearable burden on the shoulders of average citizens. The economy would be strangled, with fair competition hobbled by niggling rules and small businesses crushed beneath the weight of taxes and regulations. Worse yet, communism was abroad in the land. The permeation of this menace into American government and institutions would have dangerous effects, and perhaps even bring down democracy.

Whether or not he was fully aware of it at the time, Reagan was sounding the charge of a new conservatism. "By 1960, I realized that the real enemy wasn't big business, it was big government,"[50] Reagan wrote in his second autobiography, *An American Life*, stating succinctly what lay at the core of an incipient Republican revolution. States' rights versus the power of the federal government had always been a major plank in the conservative agenda, but the programs introduced by FDR and the changes wrought by the Second World War had given the right wing of the Republican party much more to fight against. Federal power was greater than it ever had been, and its role in American life had increased exponentially. That a vast majority of Americans seemed to approve of such programs as Social Security and Medicare did not, somehow, detract from the grassroots popularity of a view that played to deeply ingrained national values. Independence, fair competition, and freedom from regulatory constraints and heavy taxation were issues that had a wide appeal for much of America.

In 1962 Reagan made it official and registered as a member of the Republican party. Invitations to give The Speech on behalf of GE were multiplying out of control, and soon Reagan had an identity completely distinct from his movie career. He was becoming a political figure. In the year he became a Republican, Reagan ended his eight-year association with GE. "General Electric Theatre" had gone off the air in 1962, and though the company had plans to exploit Reagan's freed-up talents in a major promotional campaign, "I told them that after developing such a following by speaking out about the issues I believed in, I wasn't going to go out and peddle toasters."[51]

While the Kennedy administration presided over what would become a period of hegemony for the Democratic party, Reagan championed the Republican cause. The first step in furthering his agenda lay in propelling a conservative into office, and to that end Reagan worked hard for Barry

Goldwater in the 1964 presidential election. He gave The Speech—slightly doctored to become a campaign speech—at one Republican fund-raiser after another. When he wound up at an October 27, 1964, television broadcast of The Speech with these words—using rhetoric from both FDR and Abraham Lincoln—Reagan may have done more for his own political future than for Goldwater's:

> You and I have a rendezvous with destiny. We will preserve for our children this, the last best hope of man on earth, or we will sentence them to take the last step into a thousand years of darkness.
> We will keep in mind and remember that Barry Goldwater has faith in us. He has faith that you and I have the ability and the dignity and the right to make our own decisions and determine our own destiny.[52]

Although the party's use of this version of The Speech ultimately raised, by Reagan's account, $8 million for the campaign, Goldwater went down in flames: Lyndon Johnson won by a landslide in the 1964 election. The scale of this disaster for the Republicans was enormous. The more liberal wing of the party refused to vote for Goldwater, whose politics they felt were too extreme. An ideological rift developed that would take years to heal.

In that same year Reagan completed his last film, *The Killers,* a made-for-television remake of a 1946 movie starring Burt Lancaster. The film was based on a story by Ernest Hemingway and cast Reagan as a heavy. His performance (as always whenever he played a villain) was unconvincing, and it would have been a discouraging swan song but for a special visit Ronald and Nancy received that year. An influential Republican backer arrived at the

Nancy and Reagan
at the theater

Reagans' new Pacific Palisades ranch. His mission, on behalf of a party delegation, was to ask Reagan to run for governor of California on the Republican ticket.

At the time Reagan's chief professional responsibility was acting as host of, and occasional guest actor on, the popular television show "Death Valley Days." Now that he was no longer stumping for Goldwater, he had few other pressing obligations. He was free to throw his hat into the ring if he wanted to. Nevertheless, it was a big decision—another Rubicon in the life of Ronald Reagan.

His initial reaction was a resounding no. He later explained that he felt it was one thing to put his beliefs before the people, quite another to become embroiled in the world of politics and compromise. The Republican leadership's position was that something needed to be done to heal the schism in the party and to defeat California's entrenched two-term Democratic governor, Pat Brown. As pressure mounted for Reagan to run, Ronald and Nancy wrestled daily with the prospect. They were losing sleep. Finally it occurred to him, *"If they're right and things get worse for the party and we could have done something about it, will we ever be able to sleep at night again?"*[53]

Reagan came up with a compromise. For the next six months, until the last day of 1965, he would go on the road and give The Speech. If in that time he could find a candidate the people wanted, someone they truly desired as governor, he would use the support he had gained to campaign for that individual. As it happened, they wanted him. No other Republican contender appeared who could rival him for popular appeal, and The Speech had only worked to secure his position in the Republican limelight. On January 4, 1966, Reagan announced his candidacy for governor.

The ensuing campaign became a model of Reagan's approach to politics. A microcosm of his 1980 run for the presidency, the 1966 fight showed exactly how he would combat the classic attacks from opponents who sought to use his political inexperience and acting background against him. Typically, Reagan's response was not to cringe from these attacks or make excuses for his thespian roots; rather, he took pride in his former profession and pointed to his lack of political experience as ideal preparation for a clean sweep of government. Who better to straighten up a statehouse befouled by a Democratic dynasty than a man with no political ties, a man outside the infighting of state and party politics? After all, he had only recently joined the Republican party and had not been involved in its internecine battles. He was a man with no political past and few political debts.

Of course, this was somewhat disingenuous. Reagan was backed by powerful business and political interests, as any successful aspirant to the governorship would have to be. And he was being shaped for his new role in a manner far more clinical and scientific than had been used on any previous political candidate in history. The Behavior Sciences Corporation (BASICO) of Reseda, California, was retained to prime the inexperienced candidate to handle a political office for which few experiences thus far in life had prepared him.

But Reagan was able to find an advantage in his lack of formal preparation—and his disdain for politics as usual. When Pat Brown resorted to such low blows as a television commercial pointing out that both Abraham Lincoln's assassin

and Ronald Reagan were actors, the public began to perceive the incumbent as desperate. Better yet for Reagan, by keeping to the high ground as much as possible he was able to deploy his own Hollywood good-guy image to maximum effect. After Brown accused him of reading other people's words and acting as a figurehead for business interests, Reagan responded by making a policy of inviting questions at speaking engagements.

When all the returns were counted in the 1966 election, Reagan had defeated Brown by a margin of 58 percent to 42 percent. More striking still, the governor-elect was able to point to the support of a strong majority among middle-of-the-road voters in both parties. Although Reagan had certainly struck a chord with voters on the right edge of the spectrum, particularly in Southern California, he had also infused new blood into the party by appealing to citizens desperately seeking tax relief.

Eschewing tradition, Reagan had himself sworn in just one minute after midnight, taking control at the earliest possible moment. Pat Brown was not in attendance—there was to be nothing symbolic of smooth transition. Even the judge who swore in the new governor was not the traditional chief justice of the Supreme Court. The current holder of that office was a liberal, so Reagan prevailed upon a conservative judge to do him the honor. If the new administration had had its way, the entire ceremony would have been carried out in Southern California, where Reagan's power base lay and where most of his staff

Governor Reagan being sworn in as the thirty-third governor of California by California Supreme Court Justice Marshall McComb, Sacramento, California, 1966, holding the Bible is California Senate Chaplain Wilbur Choy

and supporters lived. But there was no getting around the move to Sacramento.

About the only downside in the Reagan household was young Patti's emotional response: She wept upon learning of her father's election. Fourteen-year-old Patti Reagan (who would later adopt her mother's maiden name of Davis) had already embarked on a lifetime of dissent that would put her on the other side of the political fence from her Republican father. Even at that young age she had been powerfully influenced by the 1960s spirit of rebellion and protest. For her, having a member of the establishment in the family was anathema and always would be.

Reagan family photo, with Patti, Nancy, Reagan, Michael, Maureen, Ron Jr., and the family dog, 1960s

Reagan's first term in the governor's office was a serious trial. The very inexperience he had pointed to as a plus also posed heady challenges. California had been touted as having the ninth-largest economy in the entire world, yet now a man with no history of governing was in charge of that economy. Reagan's staff had largely been assembled to get him into office. Once there, his people discovered a vacuum left behind by a generation of Democrats. The intricate machinery for getting things done in the capital had been dismantled. The public was awaiting big changes, but the particulars had yet to be worked out.

Once again Reagan and his team found advantages in their political inno-cence. After a series of shake-ups, the new administration came to grips with its responsibilities. Excellent staffers like William Clark began to help Reagan seize the helm. Reagan also discovered that the previous administration had had a problematic relationship with the state legislature. Rather than dealing directly with individual lawmakers, Brown had depended heavily on relationships with powerful figures within the Democratic party machinery to gain majorities and achieve his legislative ends. Because of the inevitable political squabbles and petty disgruntlements that resulted from this policy, the system had become clogged and inefficient. In bypassing this process, Reagan's crew was able to work personally with congressional figures who were delighted to have some measure of influence.

In time Reagan's first term became a success, which was a devastating surprise for many political pundits. California's welfare laws were significantly improved: The rolls were reduced and the bureaucracy was curtailed, and yet more money overall was allotted to the neediest cases. The new administration trimmed the cost of government by 10 percent. Reagan also succeeded in balancing the state's budget, which was accomplished largely through a big tax increase passed in the early days of his first term. This increase, gained without much difficulty from the newly flexible legislature, was a brilliant political move. Once the money was raised, Reagan could give it back in the form of rebates and other revenue breaks that would make California look prosperous indeed, while at the same time having money available for any programs he felt were necessary. With these achievements behind him, Reagan could face the race for a second term with some equanimity.

Reagan was not unopposed in 1970, but he might almost as well have been. The man who ran against him was Democratic powerhouse Jesse "Big Daddy" Unruh, the legislator who had brokered the tax hike for Reagan on the hunch that it might undo him politically. Technically the election should have been a true horse race, but Unruh's tactics (mostly a series of ill-timed assaults on Reagan's character and qualifications) misfired. In the words of Garry Wills:

> Unruh, like Brown before him and like every political opponent after him, found that Reagan is not merely a good campaigner himself (though he is that), but he is impossible to campaign *against.* Attacks on him always hurt the attacker, so effectively has he preengaged sympathy at many levels. As Falstaff would say, a man knows not where to have him. He is un-come-at-able. [Reagan] breezed back in.[54]

President Reagan and Nancy with Mother Teresa

Four presidents—Reagan, Ford, Carter, and Nixon—gathering at the White House prior to departing for Anwar Sadat's funeral

III. THE PRESIDENCY

From the time he was first approached to run for governor, Ronald Reagan had been considered as a potential presidential candidate. In the minds of many who backed him for office and in the dreams of a number of prominent Republicans, the governorship was to be a way station on the road to the White House. Once Reagan had acquired the experience and statesmanlike *gravitas* of high office, he would be ready for a national election.

Reagan's first bid for the highest office in the land was an abortive attempt to gain his party's nomination in 1968, just two years after his arrival in Sacramento. In this attempt Reagan was outmaneuvered by Richard Nixon, a man everyone in politics had written off in 1962, only to see him rise from the ashes and seize the nomination six years later, then the election that fall.

A closer run at the presidency followed for Reagan in 1976, on the heels of his second term as governor. This term had also gone well, priming Reagan for the office he had perhaps been seeking all along. New aides and allies had been found to help make the wheels of government turn more smoothly, and the success of the initial term had made it easier to win support for his agenda in the second.

At the Statue of Liberty celebration, July 4, 1986

1980 Republican
National Convention
with George Bush and
Gerald Ford

Throughout his governorship, Reagan had been far less controversial and far more successful in public office than even his fiercest opponents had predicted. Both he and his administration seemed to have the capacity to learn from mistakes and reshape themselves to perform the tasks at hand. This capacity remained a feature of Reagan's performance throughout his political life.

Although Reagan failed in his attempt to wrest the nomination from Gerald Ford in 1976, he did manage to establish more credibility for his candidacy than he had achieved thus far. Even so, the conservative revolution that helped propel him into office had not yet surfaced in national politics. Reagan was seen by some party idealogues at the 1976 Republican convention as a kind of relic of an earlier era, an admittedly less strident version of Goldwater, but too right wing for national politics. Still, he had received serious consideration from his party

and the full support of a growing element within it. And he was unshaken by his defeat. As his own campaign manager, John Sears, was heard to say: "'I often wondered whether Reagan could really taste defeat, the way Nixon did. Nixon had no inner confidence. But this guy did.'"[55]

Ronald and Nancy were convinced of one thing: In 1980 they would leave nothing to chance. Whatever they had learned from the past they would put into practice in one more dash for office—this time against a Democratic incumbent, Jimmy Carter.

The Reagan campaign team had always had a genius for finding an opponent's Achilles' heel. In 1976 Reagan had relentlessly castigated the Panama Canal treaty, which President Ford was then negotiating. Even though the deal had nearly been completed, Ford was compelled to ease off negotiations and perform damage control in order to get back into the race. In 1980 the issue was more obvious: Carter's weakness was the man himself and the double-digit inflation that blossomed on his watch. By portraying Carter as indecisive in his attempts to rescue the hostages in Iran and control the economy, Reagan was able to sketch a portrait of a president unable to cope with the job. Carter's hair had gone gray in office. His rhetoric had always been more realistic than uplifting. It was only natural, therefore, that the word he had used to describe the

With Gerald Ford,
June 29, 1981

effects of the previous Republican regime—*malaise*—should be applied to his own administration. The tag fit only too well. Reagan was able to campaign as the antidote, promoting a "New Beginning" without having to be overspecific about what that would entail.

Reagan had kenned that the voters were ready for new things—and a more positive rhetoric. Because he had always campaigned on the promise of sweeping change, this suited his standard approach perfectly. Although he wavered in his first debate with Carter, Reagan once again learned from his mistakes. So did his campaign team. Instead of putting the candidate through grueling briefings so he could match wits with Carter on matters an incumbent president would clearly have a better grasp of, Reagan's staff allowed him to capitalize on his own charm.

During the 1980 Presidential campaign on board the plane *Leadership 80*

With a deft quip Reagan was able to disarm Carter and seize the moment in one-on-one confrontations. Without the intense briefing sessions he was also able to relax and present his best side to the public—that of a man who understood their plight and would do what it took to get America back on track and out of the "malaise" into which Carter had sunk the country. Reagan also pointed to a "window of vulnerability," implying that Carter had cut military spending and allowed America to become an easy prey for the Soviet Union. These tactics worked. As November rolled around, the momentum for Reagan was building. Carter's polls, on the other hand, were stalling.

Reagan's massive, resounding electoral victory at the beginning of a new decade will forever stand as the end of one historic epoch and the beginning of another. Even the simple ability to hold office for two consecutive terms appeared to have vanished. For one reason or another, the five presidents previous to Reagan had failed to finish a second term. Kennedy had been assassinated, Johnson had abandoned the attempt, Nixon had been forced to resign, Ford had never been *elected* as president, and Carter had lost his second bid. Now at last America had a president with staying power.

Tip O'Neill put Reagan's victory in perspective when, despite his own staunch opposition to the winning candidate, he acknowledged that he had underestimated the depth of Reagan's popular appeal: "'People like him as an

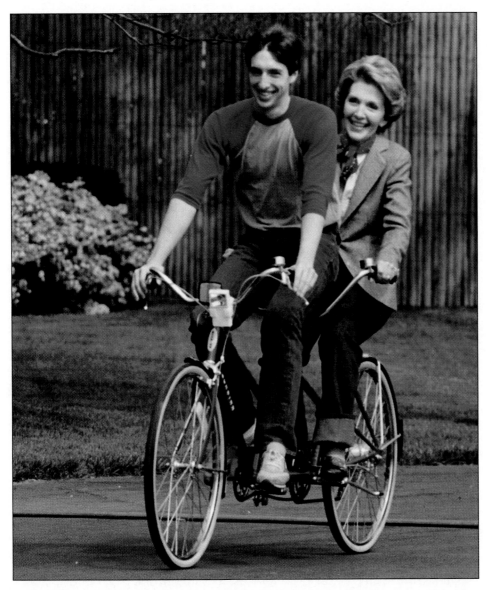

Ron Jr. and Nancy riding a tandem bicycle at the White House

individual, and he handles the media better than anybody since Franklin Roosevelt, even Jack Kennedy. . . . There's just something about the guy that people like. . . . They're rooting for him.'"[56]

From the moment of his election, Reagan began to demonstrate the new approach to government he would take. Whereas Carter had taken the $2 million allotted by the federal government to handle expenses of the interregnum and handed back change, Reagan raised an additional $2 million from private donations and put together think tanks and planning consortiums. Big things were in the wind, and Reagan was determined to seize every day up to the inauguration to ensure that change would begin rolling the minute his presidency was official.

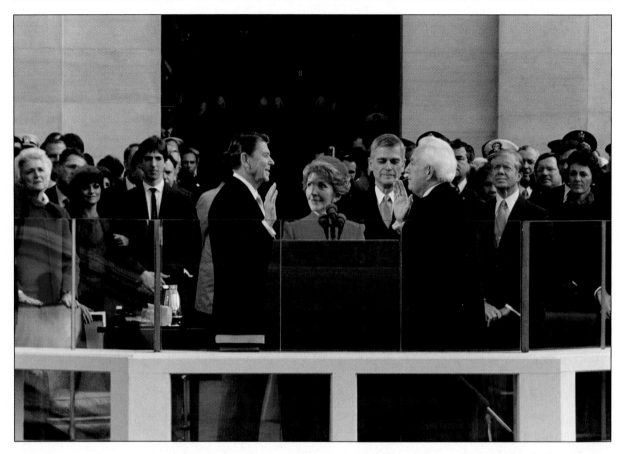

Inaugural swearing in of
President Reagan,
January 20, 1981

The inauguration itself was something special as well. The Carters had brought the formality of the White House down a notch, relating more directly to America's working classes. Ronald and (more particularly) Nancy saw that the time had come to restore a little tone to the highest office in the land. Festivities were held on a classic scale that had not been seen since the Kennedy era. Once again the Herald Trumpeters, a unit of the United States Army Band, would play "Hail to the Chief" whenever Reagan appeared. Gone was Gerald Ford's "Michigan Fight Song" and Jimmy Carter's personal anthem, "Jubilation." Elegance and stateliness swept back into the White House, but not without a few California touches. Only domestic wines would be served, and the traditional French cuisine offered at state functions would take a turn toward American tastes.

On a more profound level, at the beginning of his presidency Reagan did things that none of his recent predecessors had ever considered. First, he eschewed the notion that a new president must execute the most publicly noxious aspects of his new program within the first hundred days—the honeymoon. Reagan was determined to make changes, but not changes of this kind. His first

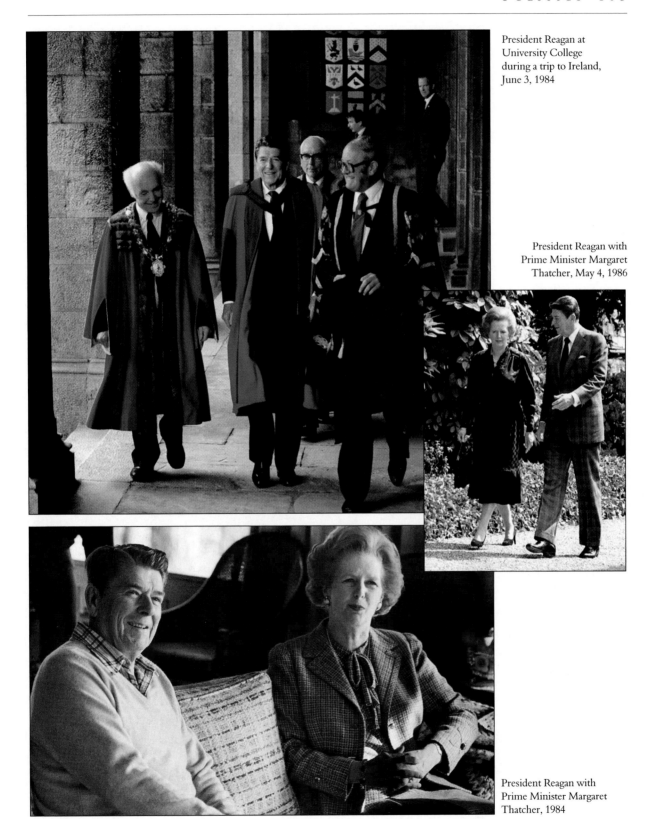

President Reagan at
University College
during a trip to Ireland,
June 3, 1984

President Reagan with
Prime Minister Margaret
Thatcher, May 4, 1986

President Reagan with
Prime Minister Margaret
Thatcher, 1984

serious proposal was a tax cut. Ronald Reagan declared open warfare on the high inflation that had helped him defeat Jimmy Carter. Moreover, Reagan made it clear to the American people that his agenda was almost exclusively domestic.

There are always plenty of problems brewing abroad, and it has traditionally been a temptation for new chief executives to embroil themselves immediately in foreign affairs. Certainly it is in visiting overseas capitals that a president can be guaranteed a show of respect and perhaps gain some inkling of his newly acquired prestige; an American president can usually find a nation that is happy to roll out the red carpet. Reagan, however, had correctly realized that the American people felt neglected. The last thing he had in mind was hopping around the globe—especially given his disinclination for travel abroad. With the exception of his occasional forays to England to make movies, he had never been outside of the United States. Now that he was president, he was determined to send the message that America and Americans were at the center of his new agenda.

Carter had concentrated on human rights all around the world, inaugurating his administration with the tremendously difficult yet successful passage of the Panama Canal treaty. He had then spent much of the rest of his first year in office preparing for the Strategic Arms Limitation Talks (SALT) negotiations.

A surprise birthday cake for President Reagan, 1983

Before him, Nixon had taken refuge in foreign policy, virtually fleeing to China and Russia to avoid the jeers and catcalls that greeted him on stateside visits. Johnson had had Vietnam. Now, at last, Americans had a president who concentrated to a great degree on them.

Certainly Reagan's first term was spent almost entirely on domestic issues. Only toward its end, in 1984, did he attend his first summit abroad. This was a trend that continued throughout the eight years of his presidency. Whether he was visiting the shores of Normandy in commemoration of the D day invasion or an economic summit in Canada (christened the Shamrock Summit by aides, to appeal to Irish Americans as they celebrated St. Patrick's Day), Reagan sought to focus attention always on America. He did not leave the country when he left the continent; instead, he found ways to bring America along in heart and mind. Not one move on a foreign visit was made without careful consideration of its political impact at home, and Reagan had carefully selected the kind of staff who could ensure that those moves were captured on television.

The heart of Reagan's domestic policy was a new economic vision that, in the first years of his administration, staggered and stalled. This novel approach to managing the nation's pocketbook acquired such labels as "supply-side" economics and "Reaganomics." By whatever name it was called, the theory stated that if the federal tax burden were lowered and business regulations pared down, the economy would expand. What happened when these economics were implemented became a subject of furious debate across the country and within the White House itself.

In the years 1981 and 1982 the nation settled into a serious recession. Reagan's own budget director, David Stockman, disagreed fundamentally with the way the country's finances were being run. He felt there was a role for taxation and regulation, albeit a reduced one. Reagan's visceral hatred for federal taxation in any form did not allow for this. Even though the nation seemed on the verge of scuppering under the influence of Reaganomics, the chief executive refused to give in to the naysayers. In time, his position was vindicated as the recession eased, then vanished, and the longest peacetime expansion of the U.S. economy in history got under way.

A LETTER TO THE PRESIDENT

Ever since his Hollywood days, Reagan had kept up a lively private correspondence with his public. This did not end when he became president. With the aid of his chief of correspondence, Anne Higgins—who had held the same office under Richard Nixon—Reagan spent at least one hour each day responding to mail from ordinary American citizens. Often the result would entail a lengthy personal response—sometimes even a small check—from Reagan himself. This correspondence was so important to the president that it was not at all uncommon for him to carry unanswered letters with him to weekends at Camp David, the presidential retreat.

For relaxation Reagan favored his own ranch at Pacific Palisades in California. There he could cut wood, ride horses, and savor the clean air far from the hothouse atmosphere of Washington. These periods of escape were vital for Reagan, who had always found rejuvenation in outdoor physical exertion. No matter where he went, however, he brought the people, and their letters, with him.

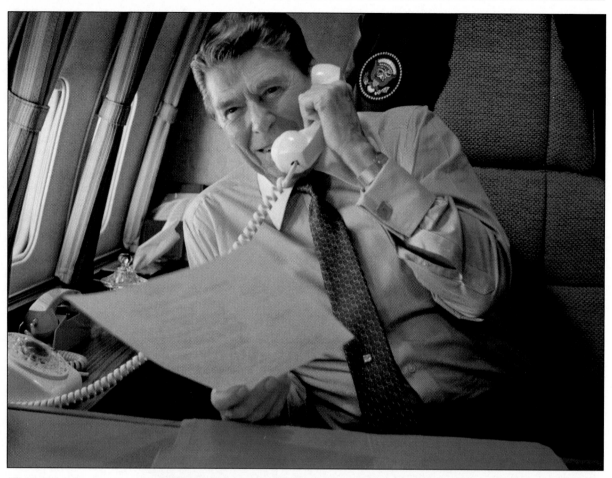

Working aboard
Air Force One

President Reagan with
Pope John Paul II,
June 6, 1987

After its rocky start, Reaganomics did indeed seem to work a miracle. The economy that had spiraled downward through the previous administration began to experience a vigorous resurgence. Suddenly Reagan's campaign rhetoric, the "Morning in America" champagne that had gone flat so soon after his election, took on new life and began to alter the general mood. This swing in public emotion was a crucial achievement of the first administration, as people began to believe in their new buying power almost before it became a reality. The stock market soared, as it continued to do throughout Reagan's two terms.

Reagan was against government waste and bureaucratic obfuscation. He seemed genuinely incensed at political abuses and actually hostile toward the kind of inside-the-beltway, professional Washington practices many Americans, blue collar and otherwise, regarded with suspicion. As William F. Buckley Jr. put it, "'[Reagan] understood the ambient circumstances, which required a high degree of intelligence and knowledge. . . . He knew, for instance, that people were afraid of inflation. He had an innate capacity to know what things people were worried about.'"[57]

President Reagan with Michael Jackson and Nancy during the 1980s

On March 30, 1981, Ronald Reagan walked out of the Hilton Hotel in Washington, D.C., having delivered a speech before the Construction Trades Council to a relatively desultory reception.

> I was almost to the car when I heard what sounded like two or three firecrackers over to my left—just a small fluttering sound, *pop, pop, pop.*
>
> I turned and said, "What the hell's that?"
>
> Just then, Jerry Parr, the head of our Secret Service unit, grabbed me by the waist and literally hurled me into the back of the limousine. I landed on my face atop the arm rest across the backseat and Jerry jumped on top of me. When he landed, I felt a pain in my upper back that was unbelievable. It was the most excruciating pain I had ever felt.
>
> "Jerry," I said, "get off, I think you've broken one of my ribs."[58]

The pain Reagan felt was not a cracked rib—it was a bullet. As he later learned while recovering from his injuries at George Washington University Hospital, a mentally deranged man named John Hinckley Jr. had opened fire on

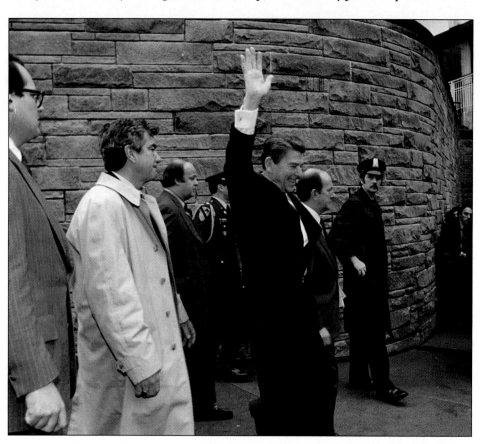

Waving to a crowd just prior to the assassination attempt, March 30, 1981

the president and his entourage. Reagan had been struck in the lung by a ricochet. Jim Brady, his press secretary, had been hit in the head, causing a wound that was at first believed to be fatal. Secret Service agent Tim McCarthy had been shot in the chest, and a policeman named Tom Delehanty had been hit in the neck. In a few terrible seconds the specter of presidential assassination had once again been raised, this time captured on videotape for the entire nation to see.

Reagan's performance that day harked back to some of his greatest achievements on screen—but not a word of it was scripted. As Reagan first came to the realization that he was severely injured (he had begun to cough up blood that foamed with bubbles, sure evidence of a lung wound), the agent who had flung himself on top of his boss shouted out orders to change the limousine's destination from the White House to the hospital. "No matter how hard I tried, I couldn't get enough air," Reagan later wrote. "I was frightened and started to panic a little." His subsequent comportment would belie this fear, to which Reagan had so characteristically confessed. Within minutes the president was on a gurney at the hospital. A nurse there held his hand as he slipped in and out of consciousness. At one point he asked her, "Does Nancy know about us?"[59]

Seconds after the assassination attempt, the president is swept off to the hospital in the limousine, March 30, 1981

President Reagan with Nancy at George Washington Hospital during his recovery after the assassination attempt, April 3, 1981

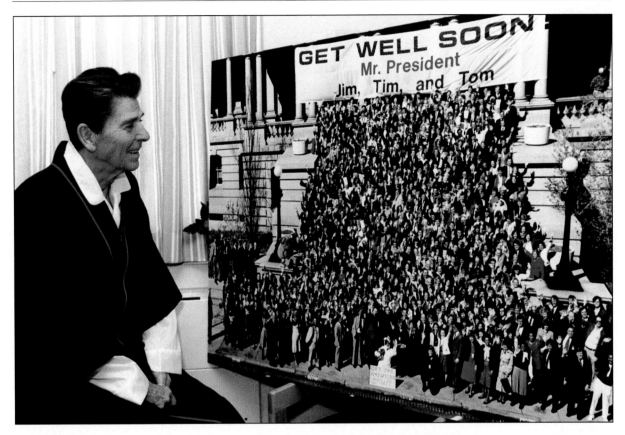

Later, as he was about to be put under anesthesia for surgery to his chest, Reagan quipped to an attending doctor, "I hope you're a Republican." The doctor responded, "Today, Mr. President, we're all Republicans."[60]

A "Get Well Soon" card received during his recovery at George Washington Hospital

The physician might have been speaking for many Americans as the public absorbed the first news of the shooting. Somehow it was Reagan himself who soothed a shocked nation with his easy demeanor and ready wit. "Honey, I forgot to duck,"[61] Reagan told Nancy when he first regained consciousness. It was a quotation from Jack Dempsey, who had used the same words to his own wife after being nailed by Gene Tunney in a heavyweight boxing championship.

Jokes aside, Reagan's shooting initiated the most severe crisis his administration had faced thus far. The most powerful individual in the world had been incapacitated and nearly killed. The fact that Reagan emerged the hero of the episode—overshadowing even the bodyguard who had thrown himself directly in the line of fire and taken a bullet in the chest—testifies to his ability to keep his nerve even under extreme duress. Literally as long as he was conscious, Reagan was demonstrating a suave cool that camouflaged the true seriousness of the event. And just as with his own account of his lifeguarding heroics, Reagan's description of the shooting downplayed his role. He did not boast. Indeed he

made reference to his own fear. Once again Reagan emerged as self-deprecating hero, the master of the moment who can find the words needed to make everything seem all right. And this time, no one could accuse him of reading cue cards.

After the shooting Reagan enjoyed an enormous boost in popularity, six months of positive opinion polls that amounted to a new honeymoon for his nascent administration. As 1982 gave way to 1983, the economy also began to heat up and the recession receded, adding to Reagan's newfound momentum. Only in 1983 did the Reagan Revolution, as some were calling it, hit a brick wall.

Although Reagan's economic "miracle" loomed large among the achievements of his first term in office, 1983 brought a whirlwind of dilemmas, both political and otherwise. No matter how rosy the domestic fiscal picture might become, affairs on other shores moved outside of Reagan's control and occasionally took on a life of their own.

In 1982 the United States began to be sucked into a quagmire developing in Lebanon. Israel had invaded its neighboring country in retaliation for a series of missile attacks on its own territory. The situation was a classic Middle East political nightmare involving a vast array of feuding parties, and as U.S. Marines became more and more exposed, the nation began to express its fears. Although Reagan stood firmly against sending American troops to Nicaragua (knowing that, despite his belief in the contras, such a move would be political suicide), he committed soldiers to the Middle East on the principle that since the United States had handed back the Panama Canal the nation had appeared to be on the retreat. Reagan wanted to demonstrate some military resolve in a region in which stability was crucial to world peace.

At the same time, he was keenly aware of a possible parallel with Vietnam. The president publicly announced that America's interests were at stake in Lebanon. Nevertheless, his popularity declined, bot-

CENTRAL AMERICA

Since his days as head of the Screen Actors Guild, Ronald Reagan had been an ardent enemy of communism. When he took office in January 1981, Reagan found a focus for his opposition almost as close to home as the communists of 1940s Hollywood—and to the eyes of many in his administration, far more of a menace.

In 1979 Augusto Sandino, a hero of Nicaraguan revolutionaries, had overthrown the military regime of Anastasio Somoza. Although Jimmy Carter had initially provided the Sandinista government with aid, the United States soured on Nicaragua when that country's troops invaded the neighboring country of El Salvador. Carter sent military advisers and financial aid to Jose Napoleon Duarte, El Salvador's democratic leader. It seemed the time for a showdown with communism was at hand.

Ronald Reagan moved cautiously in Central America at first, and he was wary of sending American troops into another jungle embroglio. Both he and the military were well aware of the legacy of Vietnam, so the initial position of his administration was simply to continue support for El Salvador. But Reagan was convinced that the communist threat, bankrolled in Nicaragua and other Central American countries by nearby Cuba, was real. Ultimately the Reagan administration backed a group of guerrilla fighters who were trying to topple the Sandinistas. Known as *contras* (or counterrevolutionaries), these insurgents received military aid and training from the United States. Yet the idea of extending that commitment never took hold.

toming out after a terrorist succeeded in killing 241 Marines in Beirut with a single car bomb on October 23, 1983. FBI specialists later determined that the device had delivered the largest non-nuclear blast on record, the equivalent of twelve thousand pounds of TNT. It was also the largest blow Reagan received in his first term, more devastating by far than the bullet that had struck him in 1981.

After the bombing of the Marine headquarters and its resulting political fallout, the dramatic invasion of Grenada in October 1983 supplied some needed relief for the Reagan administration. The rationale provided for the invasion was that this small Caribbean island was a possible staging area for Cuban (and hence communist) support of the Sandinista government in Nicaragua. The chief evidence for this was that U.S. spy satellites had detected an airstrip on Grenada far larger than necessary for such an island of so few inhabitants. In addition, there was an American medical school located there, conceivably putting U.S. citizens at risk. It was the cornerstone of Reagan's Central America policy to halt any attempts by Cuba to aid the spread of communism in this hemisphere. Decisive action was called for and the resulting invasion of Grenada was a success.

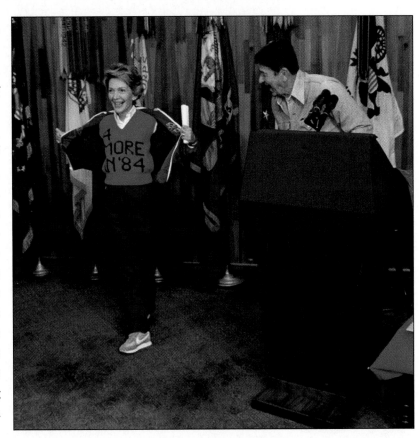

Nancy helps President Reagan announce his bid for reelection. "4 more in '84," October 6, 1984

Reagan's hold on the White House was only confirmed by the 1984 landslide election, a ringing endorsement of the Reagan vision. Walter Mondale had taken his best shot and failed to dent the president's armor; his home state of Minnesota provided the only electoral votes the Democratic challenger was to receive. Even Massachusetts and Washington, D.C., two famous Democratic strongholds, failed to support him. A nation that felt itself brimming with economic health and a business community enjoying a fiscal feast unparalleled since the years immediately following the Second World War were not about to let Reagan go.

President Reagan debates
Walter Mondale, 1984

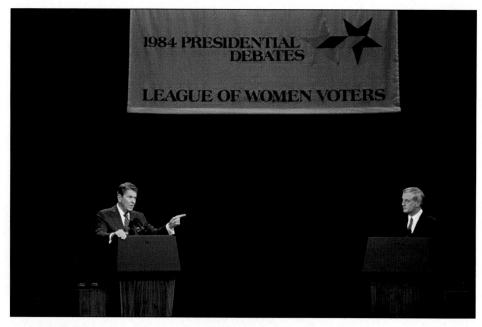

Nancy with son, Ron,
at the 1984 Republican
National Convention,
August 22, 1984

The decision to run for a second term had not been a knee-jerk affair. A man of seventy-three, Reagan was feeling the strain of the presidency. Still, it was Nancy and not Ronald who was having second thoughts. She knew only too well what another term might exact from both of them. After much searching discussion with Nancy, Reagan decided to run. There was still work to be done.

Reagan's focus necessarily altered as the world underwent a series of radical changes in his second term. Cracking like ice on a lake frozen for over sixty years, the great socialist experiment called the Soviet Union was beginning to buckle. Ronald Reagan had been fighting communism for nearly four decades, and although the crumbling and eventual collapse of the Soviet Union cannot be ascribed solely to him, it is probable that no one else could have so thoroughly exploited the opportunities presented. The Soviets admitted to shooting down a Korean jetliner that resulted in the deaths of several hundred people, including many Americans. Even before that, Reagan had called the Soviet Union an "Evil Empire." As strong as it was, this rhetoric was a shock to the Soviet leadership. It had been a long time since an American president had used such forceful language against the Russians. And yet the very forthrightness of his speech bolstered Reagan's bargaining power with

President Reagan and
Vice President Bush
at the 1984 Republican
National Convention,
August 22, 1984

those same leaders. They understood tough speech and tended to believe in it. America, for once, was being led by someone who matched the tone of political discourse in the Soviet Union, pointing to ideology and not *realpolitik* as a basis for action.

Although Carter had not neglected defense spending, as Reagan often implied in the heat of his first campaign, the new Republican administration had increased it considerably. The advent of the Strategic Defense Initiative (SDI) had put into Reagan's hands a whole new bargaining tool. In essence, the SDI was a plan for defending the United States through a new form of technology. In its original conception, the SDI employed satellite-mounted lasers that would be capable of blasting incoming Soviet intercontinental ballistic missiles right out of the sky. Later incarnations of the plan involved the use of such high-tech developments as "brilliant pebbles," hordes of tiny smart bombs, also deployed in space, that would seek out and destroy enemy missiles.

Swearing in ceremonies
for President Reagan,
January 21, 1985

Inaugural family portrait,
1985
Front row, left to right:
Beth Reagan, Neil Reagan,
Ashley Reagan, Ronald
Reagan, Nancy Reagan,
Doria Reagan, Anne Davis,
Patricia Davis
Back row, left to right:
Maureen Reagan, Dennis
Revell, Michael Reagan,
Colleen Reagan, Patti Davis,
Ronald Reagan, Jr., Geoffrey
Davis, Richard Davis
Standing in front of Ronald
Reagan is Cameron Reagan.

REYKJAVÍK—TEN HOURS THAT CHANGED HISTORY

From October 11 to 12, 1986, Iceland's tiny capital of Reykjavík played host to a decisive moment in world history. For decades the Soviet Union and the United States had been at loggerheads over the issue of nuclear arms. As the race to build ever greater stockpiles of atomic weapons continued unabated, efforts to diminish those deadly armories sputtered and died in one summit after another. By the summer of 1986, the deadlock in Geneva was deader than ever. In July, the new Russian leader, Mikhail Gorbachev, sent Ronald Reagan a letter. Its substance was that a new "major impulse" was required from the leaders of the two superpowers if there was to be any prospect of ensuring the safety of the world from nuclear destruction.

Although he adhered to a doctrine of national strength, Ronald Reagan had always been a great believer in ultimate nuclear disarmament. For decades the U.S. policy had been one of deterrence, using nuclear weapons to counterbalance the Soviet threat. To Reagan, viewing atomic bombs as counters in a complicated standoff was unthinkable; unilateral disarmament was equally illogical. For him, the Strategic Defense Initiative was the answer. By developing an impregnable system of defense against nuclear attack, the president felt he could ensure the safety of the American people while eliminating recourse to nuclear attack on the part of the Soviets. Reagan brought the SDI with him to the bargaining table in Reykjavík, and it proved decisive.

The president arrived in Iceland on October 9. Like prizefighters before a bout in the ring, both he and Gorbachev were aggressively courted by the media. When Gorbachev arrived the next day, Reagan cracked aloud as he watched the television coverage, "When you stop trying to take over the world, then maybe we can do some business" (Lou Cannon, *President Reagan: The Role of a Lifetime* [New York: Simon & Schuster, 1991], 765). Demonstrating both a tough resolve and a respect for his own role as only one of two parties to the negotiation, the president set the stage for a remarkable encounter.

Just ten hours after the negotiations had begun, Ronald Reagan stormed out of the summit. Both leaders had arrived in an aggressive frame of mind. Gorbachev was committed to the Antiballistic Missile treaty, which barred any form of antinuclear defense. Reagan was adamant about the deployment of the SDI. Both men sought the elimination of intermediate-range nuclear missiles in Europe—which Reagan referred to as the "Zero Option." For him, it was a step toward the total elimination of nuclear armaments. By Sunday afternoon a substantial reduction in missiles had been agreed upon. But when Gorbachev called Reagan on the SDI, Reagan didn't blink. He walked out.

"As Reagan put his coat on, Gorbachev said, 'can't we do something about this,'" Lou Cannon later recounted. "Reagan had had enough. 'It's too late,' he said" (Cannon, *President Reagan,* 769).

Ronald Reagan refused to budge on what he so firmly believed in as the only defense left to the United States. When he did so, the Soviet leadership was left with the definite impression that the SDI was real and that the American president was a tough customer.

President Reagan at the Geneva Summit. This was the first meeting between Reagan and Mikhail Gorbachev.

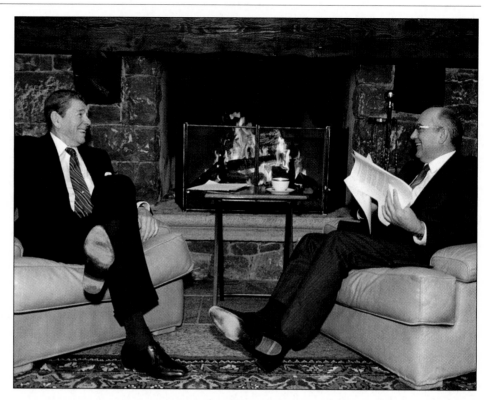

This new technology had not yet been perfected. Many experts argued that it never would be. But whichever camp of pundits one believed in—the scientists who said that "Star Wars," as they derisively called it, was unworkable and impossible or those who believed it was the wave of the future—the Soviet Union's leaders reacted on the assumption that it would be a devastatingly effective defensive weapon. As a result, Reagan could gain points by offering to refuse to build a weapons system he might not have been able to commission in the first place. For this, Soviet leader Mikhail Gorbachev was prepared to offer real concessions as Reagan's INF and START discussions began to chalk up genuine, substantive achievements in foreign policy. With the signing of the INF treaty on December 8, 1987, an entire class of nuclear weapons was eliminated for the first time in history. That achievement had resulted from a shaky summit with Gorbachev in Reykjavík, Iceland, at which Reagan had stalked out after ten hours of discussion. Again, these were dramatics the Soviets could understand, even if they flew in the face of decades of evenhanded negotiation. The walkout had been an ice breaker, and the SDI was the ice pick.

Reagan's role in weakening the Soviet Union and, ultimately, in reducing the threat of nuclear annihilation for the people of both nations was one of his proudest achievements. The economic recovery had represented the realization of one set of dreams, perhaps extending back to his own early memories of near

President Reagan and
Nancy with Governor
and Hillary Clinton,
February 22, 1987

impoverishment and rescue at the hands of another president. But the issue of nuclear arms had awakened in Reagan a still deeper call to the heroic role for which he had been preparing himself throughout his life.

Reagan's passion for the SDI was one evidence of his revulsion for nuclear conflict. Just as he felt he must confront the Soviets with a tough stance that betrayed no willingness to back down, so he felt that once a single missile flew either way the result would be disaster for both sides. Any approach to arms reduction that did not have the utter eradication of nuclear weapons at its heart did not make sense to him.

By concentrating on "Star Wars," Reagan introduced a new element to the equation, one that in the end may have tipped the balance toward the "Zero Option" of mutual disarmament. By staunchly refusing even to pretend that the SDI was a bargaining chip, Reagan turned it into the best chip imaginable. Yet the president also tipped his own hand. Reagan the hero saw himself as raising a great technological protective shield above the people he loved better than any on earth.

Thus it was in carrying out the highest, most important task of his presidency—securing the world, and most of all the American people, from nuclear war—that Ronald Reagan rounded out his second and final term of office.

When the Marine helicopter lifted off from behind the great dome of the Capitol on January 20, 1989, Reagan marveled at the ease with which the peaceful transition of power takes place in America. He might well have wondered, too, at the seeming ease of the transitions that had brought him to where he was—from campus hero to radio announcer to movie star to governor to revered former president. He and Nancy were being ferried one last time to catch a flight on what for eight years had been Air Force One. Their destination was California and the Reagans' beloved ranch.

Just as Reagan's assumption of the responsibilities of California's governorship had defied strident predictions of disaster, so his presidency rose to the challenges it faced. Again and again potential pitfalls had become springboards to new heights. And just as the attempt on his life by the demented assailant John Hinckley Jr. ultimately proved a showcase for Reagan's grit and calm in the face of disaster—his poise would become legend as he quipped his way into the operating room—so serious attempts to deflate his popularity met stony resistance on the part of the public. The people finally had a hero on their hands. They were not about to let that slip away.

It had always been the persistence of Reagan's vision, his irreducible drive to achieve a set of goals based on firm convictions, that had set him apart. This commitment to higher ideals, allied to a power base that helped push many of his beliefs into law, adorned Reagan with the kind of heroic laurels that he had both won and downplayed throughout a

"HE DID NOT NEED A SCRIPT"

One of the more remarkable sides to Ronald Reagan's character is also the least known: his compassion. He received hundreds of letters throughout his terms of office, from close friends, political enemies, and ordinary citizens alike. When they wrote to him about sorrow and loss, Reagan seemed to have a special gift for bringing comfort in an intimate, humane way. In his 1991 book *President Reagan: The Role of a Lifetime* (New York: Simon & Schuster), Reagan biographer Lou Cannon recalled how the president exhibited remarkable empathy on a tragic occasion:

> He called me at home after my mother died in 1983. Her death seemed merciful, for she had been ill a long time, but I was surprised how little I had been prepared for it. When I said as much to Reagan, he responded, "You are never prepared for the death of your mother," then proceeded to tell me his feelings when his own mother had died under similar circumstances. I was consoled and overcome. In such moments he did not need a script (178).

Characteristically, Reagan's last phone call from the Oval Office was delivered to someone in distress. His desk bare, the office empty, he picked up the telephone and had a call put through to the home of his loyal aide, Lyn Nofziger. Nofziger's eldest daughter, Sue Piland, was dying of cancer. Later, Reagan's personal secretary sent a photograph of the president to the Nofzigers, showing the man as he cradled the phone and did what he could to ease the suffering of Nofziger's wife.

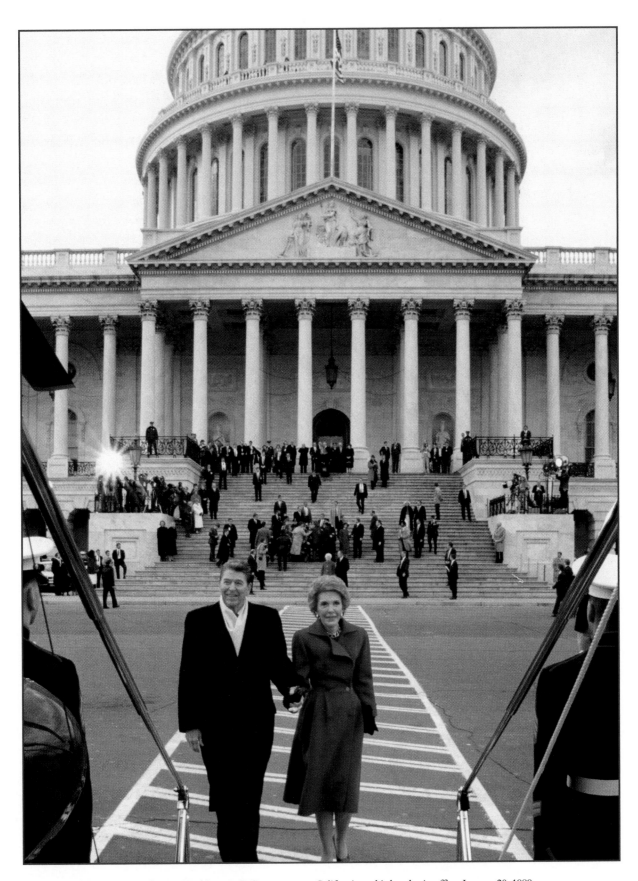

President and Nancy Reagan leaving Washington, D.C., on route to California on his last day in office, January 20, 1989

lifetime of achievement. Reagan believed in seizing the day. He did it at that first student strike at Eureka, again at WHO in Des Moines, and yet again in Hollywood and Sacramento. Rarely in American life has there been a man who better understood the tenor of his own times and who could grasp more quickly the essence of the problems at hand.

There is, of course, more to it than that. Chances come to those who look for them. Perhaps no one in politics has ever believed more thoroughly in his own personal star than Ronald Reagan. The sweat never seemed to show, as it so definitely had with many of his immediate predecessors. It was this confidence that won him his following, and it was the depth of his belief that allowed him to stay the course and make a reality of his many dreams.

President Reagan and Nancy at their ranch

Reagan at work in his Century City office, May 18, 1995

Notes

PROLOGUE

1. Tip O'Neill and William Novak, *Man of the House: The Life and Political Memoirs of Speaker Tip O'Neill* (New York: Random House, 1987), p. 363.
2. Evan Thomas, "Every Region, Every Age Group, Almost Every Voting Bloc," *Time,* November 19, 1984, p. 45.
3. Lou Cannon, *President Reagan: The Role of a Lifetime* (New York: Simon & Schuster, 1991), p. 494.
4. Cannon, *President Reagan,* p. 275.

EARLY YEARS

5. Ronald Reagan, *An American Life* (New York: Simon and Schuster, 1990), p. 21.
6. Ronald Reagan and Richard G. Hubler, *Where's the Rest of Me?* (New York: Dell Publishing Company, Inc., 1965), p. 18.
7. Reagan, *Where's the Rest of Me?*, p. 15.
8. Ibid., p. 16.
9. Ibid., p. 16.
10. Ibid., p. 17.
11. Ibid., p. 17.
12. Anne Edwards, *Early Reagan: The Rise to Power* (New York: William Morrow and Company, Inc., 1987), p. 38.
13. Edwards, *Early Reagan,* p. 40.
14. Ibid., p. 39.
15. Reagan, *Where's the Rest of Me?*, p. 13.
16. Ibid., p. 23.
17. Garry Wills, *Reagan's America: Innocents at Home* (New York: Doubleday & Company, Inc., 1987), p. 29.
18. Reagan, *Where's the Rest of Me?*, p. 28.
19. Ibid., p. 23–24.

AMBITION

20. Ibid., p. 36–37.
21. Reagan, *An American Life*, p. 57.
22. Edwards, *Early Reagan,* p. 102.
23. Reagan, *Where's the Rest of Me?*, p. 109–110.
24. Ibid., p. 54.
25. Ibid., p. 57–58.
26. Ibid., p. 58–59.
27. Ibid., p. 60.
28. Ibid., p. 61.
29. Edwards, *Early Reagan,* p. 119.
30. Reagan, *An American Life*, p. 70.
31. Edwards, *Early Reagan,* p. 141.
32. Ibid., p. 144.
33. Reagan, *Where's the Rest of Me?*, p. 79.
34. Edwards, *Early Reagan,* p. 138.
35. Reagan, *Where's the Rest of Me?*, p. 82.

THE MOVIES

36. Ibid., p. 84.
37. Ibid., p. 85.
38. Ibid., p. 85–86.
39. Ibid., p. 87.
40. Reagan, *An American Life*, p. 81.
41. Ibid., p. 81.
42. Ibid., p. 86.
43. Reagan, *Where's the Rest of Me?*, p. 118.
44. Edwards, *Early Reagan*, p. 193.
45. Reagan, *Where's the Rest of Me?*, p. 154.
46. Ibid., p. 150–151.
47. Ibid., p. 147.
48. Wills, *Reagan's America*, p. 236.
49. Edwards, *Early Reagan*, p. 370.

POLITICS

50. Reagan, *An American Life*, p. 135.
51. Ibid., p. 137.
52. Ibid., p. 142–143.
53. Ibid., p. 146.
54. Wills, *Reagan's America*, p. 312.
55. Ibid., p. 331.
56. Cannon, *President Reagan*, p. 116.
57. Ibid., p. 134.
58. Reagan, *An American Life*, p. 259.
59. Ibid., p. 260.
60. Ibid., p. 261.
61. Ibid., p. 260.

DESIGNER'S NOTE

THE TEXT OF THIS BOOK WAS SET IN BEMBO, THE DISPLAY IN COPPERPLATE GOTHIC
BY SNAP-HAUS GRAPHICS OF EDGEWATER, NJ.

BOOK DESIGN BY DIANE STEVENSON OF SNAP-HAUS GRAPHICS